P9-DYD-354

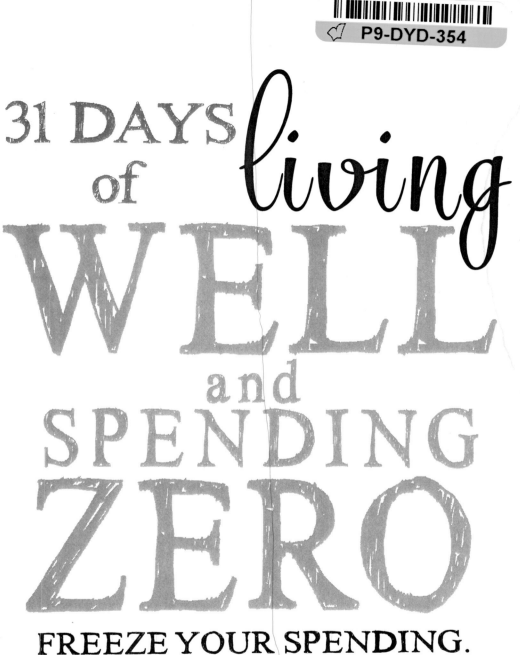

31 DAYS of *living* WELL and SPENDING ZERO

FREEZE YOUR SPENDING. CHANGE YOUR LIFE.

RUTH SOUKUP

LIFE WELL LIVED PUBLICATIONS
31 Days of Living Well and Spending Zero
Copyright © 2015 by Ruth Soukup
This title is also available as an eBook for Kindle
Visit www.LivingWellSpendingLess.com/shop

Requests for information should be addressed to:
Life Well Lived Publishing, 207 Cross Street, Suite 302 Punta Gorda, FL 33950

Library of Congress Cataloging-in-Publication Data
Soukup, Ruth, 1978-
31 Days of Living Well and Spending Zero/Ruth Soukup.
pages cm
ISBN 0692483365 (paperback)
1. Finance, Personal. 2. Budgets, Personal. 3. Saving and investment.

Any Internet addresses (websites, blogs, etc) in this book are offered as a resource. They are not intended in any way to be or imply an endorsement by Life Well Lived Publications, nor does Life Well Lived vouch for the content of these sites for the life of this book.

All rights reserved. No part of this publication may be reproduced, stored in a retrieval system, or transmitted in any form or by any means—electronic, mechanical, photocopy, recording, or any other—except for brief quotations in printed reviews, without the prior permission of the publisher.

Cover design: Bree Dillow-Moss
Printed in the United States of America
ISBN: 0692483365
ISBN 13: 9780692483367

31 Days of Living Well and Spending Zero
Freeze Your Spending. Change Your Life.

Ruth Soukup
www.LivingWellSpendingLess.com

LIFE
WELL
LIVED
PUBLICATIONS

Table of Contents

Week 5: The Final Stretch: Create Lasting Change

Introduction

Welcome to 31 Days of Living Well and Spending Zero!

You are about to embark on a month that will stretch you and challenge you. You'll be kick-starting your budget and overhauling your spending patterns. Initially it sounds simple—just don't spend money. That's it. But let's be honest—while most of us do our best to keep our spending in check, we often go off track, despite our best intentions. Sometimes a reboot is in order, and a no-spend month is a great opportunity to not only reset your patterns, but to really dig deep and find areas for savings that we may not have considered before.

So how much money can you save in a month?

Truthfully, it depends on how much you normally spend. Every family's budget is a little different, so how much you save will depend largely on how much you are currently spending. If you are already sacrificing and going without, this challenge probably won't be a magic cure, but it may very well give you renewed focus and hope, as well as some fantastic ideas for how to stretch your dollars even further.

On the other hand, if you are currently in a pattern of frequent and frivolous spending—eating out, daily stops at Starbucks, frequent treks to Target or the mall, or online shopping on Amazon.com—taking a month off could mean saving upwards of $1,000 or more.

In any case, taking a conscious break from spending and a long hard look at your spending patterns and bank account will help you make positive changes to your financial life, no matter where you are in the journey. We'll get started right away on Day 1, assessing where you are and determining what areas you may be able to cut back on.

Once you assess your budget, you might be surprised to find areas where your spending is adding up to more than you realized. Maybe it's a magazine habit or a daily stop at the gas station on the way to work for a cup of coffee. Perhaps you and your husband resort to takeout or fast food several times a week because you're both just too tired to cook. Eating out is definitely one of the biggest budget busters out there—and one that often adds up quickly. That's why the first week of our challenge starts with making a plan for what you will eat all month. If you employ just a little resourcefulness, you might be surprised at how easy it is to eat at home, even when you're tired or busy.

After we get our kitchens on a budget in *Week 1: Get Started and Plan Your Meals*, we'll start to explore the rest of our homes in *Week 2: Clean and Organize*. The fact is, it is much easier to keep your spending in check when you stay home more, and it's much nicer to be at home when your home is clean. Not only that, but you may even find a few treasures you'd forgotten about. By paring down, simplifying, and getting a handle on all your family's "stuff," you'll find renewed appreciation for all that you already have.

During *Week 3: Flex Your Creativity*, we'll work on getting those creative juices flowing and discover all the things we can make, do, learn, and create ... for free. Not spending money doesn't mean sitting at home reading library books by candlelight. (Although that can actually be fun once in a while!) You can do a surprising number of fun, creative activities; learn new things; and even "treat yourself" without spending a dime.

By the time we reach *Week 4: Earn Money and Enjoy Freebies*, we'll practically be savings superstars—and, believe it or not, you may even find you're enjoying this challenge! In Week 4, we'll explore ways to earn a little extra money and get free goods and services. Plus, we'll discover great ways to enjoy fun and free family time—and we'll even treat ourselves to a date night!

Each week includes a day of self-reflection. Looking back and reflecting upon the changes you are making is an important part of the process, so I highly recommend that you don't skip this part! After all, our goal is change that lasts, right?

This 31 Days of Living Well and Spending Zero challenge was originally started in 2012, and in the years since, tens of thousands of Living Well Spending Less readers have taken it—many more than once. Throughout this process, I'll share both advice from other readers and tips and tricks I've learned along the way. You'll discover ways to get your family on board and ensure everyone learns something new—while having fun doing it.

At the end of our journey, we'll finish strong by looking at ways to keep the ball rolling once our no-spend month is over. They say the best and most long-lasting diets are really lifestyle changes, not just temporary sacrifices. Learning how to have a healthy wallet is no different. By month's end, we will have learned more than a few practices and habits to help us live with less and appreciate what we have all the more. And in the end, isn't that what living the good life is really all about?

It is never fun to feel like you are in it alone, and for this challenge, you definitely are not alone. Every month thousands of LWSL readers recommit to Living Well and Spending Zero, which means that there is almost certainly someone, somewhere, going through the same struggles that you are. We encourage you to share updates and photos of your progress on Instagram, Twitter, or Facebook using hashtag #31DaysLWSZ so that others can share in your journey.

And now, without further ado, please join me for 31 Days of Living Well and Spending Zero!

> I'm looking forward to this month. We usually do our no-spend month in February—this upcoming one will be our fifth year.   - Debra

week
ONE

get
STARTED
& PLAN *meals*
YOUR

Day 1: **Get Started**

The first time my husband suggested a month of no spending, back in 2012, I thought he was crazy. After all, by that point we had been married six years, and if he knew only one thing about me, it was that I liked to shop. Like many families, we were caught in a pattern of unhealthy spending habits.

It wasn't that we were constantly out spending wildly on big-ticket items, but our little daily habits were killing us. With two small kids at home, I'd often go to Target just to get out of the house. Of course a trip to Target also meant a stop at Starbucks and lunch at Chick-Fil-A, and then, because I was tired from a day of running around, it often meant ordering pizza or grabbing Chinese takeout on the way home.

While we weren't in debt, we weren't making any headway either. Every penny that came in, we spent. Something had to give.

We decided that we would challenge ourselves to an entire month of no spending. No eating out. No Starbucks. No Amazon. com. And definitely no Target. Furthermore, we would have to eat the food we already had stored up in our pantry and freezer. After all, I was really great at grocery shopping, but not always so great at actually using the food I had on hand. We would still pay our regular bills and our mortgage, but anything we could cut out, we would. For an entire month.

It was life changing.

I would have never guessed that 31 days of no spending could make such a significant difference in the way I viewed my finances, but it did. In the years since, we have continued to commit regularly to no-spend months, usually about twice a year.

In that time, I've gathered quite a few tips and tricks along the way to make things a little easier, not only from my own experiences but also from many wonderful LWSL readers (just like you!).

Get Ready to Commit

I have discovered that once you decide to embark on a no-spend month, there is a very important first step: to commit.

This is the day we will change the way we look at spending. This is the day we will stop making excuses and stop justifying yet one more purchase. This is the day we will, for one whole month, commit to spending nothing.

Are you ready?

Right here, right now, I want you to fully commit to this month of living well and spending zero. Say the words out loud, preferably to your spouse and to your kids. Make it real.

Is it hard?

I'm not going to lie—at first it might be tough. But there is a secret to success. You have to be in—fully in, going head first and full force! (If you're married, be sure your spouse is on board too.) You can't go into this challenge half-heartedly or you will fail. That's why we've included a commitment sheet for you to sign at the end of this chapter!

In my family's very first round of this experiment we definitely longed for a few luxury items. By the third day I really, really regretted that I didn't stock up on a few bottles of wine, and about halfway through the month I might have traded both my children for just one double -tall-one-and-a-half-pump-cinnamon-dolce latte. We ate more than a few very random—and not in a good way—meals, and we sometimes found ourselves talking longingly about all the favorite restaurants we used to frequent. My oldest daughter Maggie literally counted down the days until we could go back to the Golden Corral. (Yep, we really know how to live!)

But in the end, I was amazed to find we saved over $1,000. We found resources we had long since forgotten. We found items in the pantry we'd overlooked. We found toys that had been discarded. We certainly found creativity that we had stifled.

> I did a spending freeze last year and it was fabulous! So empowering to have the ability to just say no to buying the inessentials! —Laurie

I wish I could say we didn't fight about money that whole time, but in a strange twist, we actually had a doozy of a fight when my husband wanted to spend a few dollars on something and I said no, that it wasn't "essential." (Let me tell you, having had all our previous money fights originate from my poor spending habits, it was practically like The Twilight Zone to have it go the other way.) But we lived!

And when someone asked, at the end of the month, would we do it again, our answer was an emphatic yes! In fact, we've now gone through a handful of rounds of spending zero, and every time we do it, we gain new insights and greater appreciation for everything we already have. We have a life rich with faith, family, friends, and creativity. We've learned to be secure in the idea that a life well lived has nothing to do with what we have, but instead is made of who we are and what we do with what's been given to us.

Establishing GROUND Rules:

Once you've signed your commitment, it's time to set up the ground rules for your month. For us it was pretty simple: no spending on anything that wasn't absolutely essential.

For our family that meant giving money to church, paying our regular bills and utilities, and some essentials (like a can't-wait car repair). The only food we allowed ourselves to purchase over the month included bread, milk, eggs, and cheese. The rest of our food came from our pantry and freezer. (Yes, it was a challenge.)

Of course, I think one of the things that holds people back from actually committing is the fear that there is never a "good" month to make it happen. Every month, it seems, has some sort of special circumstance— a vacation, a birthday, a holiday. How do you work around those?

The key is accounting for those special circumstances and planning for them ahead of time. I've included a worksheet at the end of this chapter that can help you do just that.

> For those essentials like milk, and the essential items I get weekly, I'm going to load up my grocery budget on a gift card so I won't be tempted to go over. — Kim

Some of our readers have mentioned that they have been tempted to stockpile items before starting the challenge. If you have genuine concerns about essentials (yes, you can still buy toilet paper), you can start with a very limited trip to the store or allow yourself a minimal allotment for the basics ($25 or so should keep you covered). Assess what you have on hand, and remember: even if you're spending the whole month eating mostly pasta or rice, you can make it.

Don't procrastinate and wait for the "perfect month" to begin, because there will never be a perfect month! If you have commitments like a big family event coming up, view the event as a challenge in your plan, get creative, and move on. A friend of mine made a sock monkey for a birthday gift, homemade valentines and an eggless cake, and still managed to make it through February just fine without spending a thing. The perfect month will never happen, so rather than putting it off, take the plunge!

> We have a birthday (my son's) this month, but we've already bought his gift. We have a very small party planned (going to a local farm), but the money was set aside for that already. — Liz

Create your own ground rules that account for your circumstances, and find the best ways to make your no-spend month work for you and your family. If you have an empty freezer and pantry, yes, you might have to do a little shopping beforehand, but keep it frugal and plan for the month.

There are a few expenses you can definitely cut out for the month:

- Eating out at restaurants
- Coffee from coffee shops
- Clothing
- Hobbies—crafts, golf, classes, etc.
- Entertainment
- Toys
- Cosmetics and sundries
- Alcohol and other vices
- Lottery tickets
- Furniture and home décor

What else can you add to this list right now?

GROUND rules

FREEZE YOUR SPENDING CHANGE YOUR LIFE

spending
FREEZE

_____

**GROCERY OR TOILETRY ITEMS
I/WE MAY BUY THIS MONTH:**

Other THOUGHTS

**THINGS I/WE HAVE COMMITTED TO
PAYING FOR THIS MONTH:**

**THINGS I/WE MAY ABSOLUTELY
NOT PURCHASE THIS MONTH:**

Copyright · Living Well Spending Less Inc · www.LivingWellSpendingLess.com

The closer it got to starting our month of no spending,
the more nervous I got, but now that it is finally here,
I am excited! We have gotten very careless with
our spending lately and I am ready to get back on
track! — Dawn

Ready to commit? Excited to get started? Once you've signed your commitment sheet snap a picture and tweet it or share it on Instagram with the hashtag #31DaysLWSZ!

I

Being of sound body and mind, do solemnly commit to **31 days of Living Well & Spending Zero**. During this time I will limit my variable expenditures to **ONLY** those deemed absolutely necessary for survival, per the ground rules of this challenge.

Signed this   day of   , 20

Signature

MY *commitment*

FREEZE YOUR SPENDING. CHANGE YOUR LIFE.

Copyright © Living Well Spending Less, Inc. www.LivingWellSpendingLess.com

Finally, throughout this challenge, there will be many different worksheets and printables for you to use. I suggest you print them out and organize them together in a binder or folder so you can journal as you go. You can access a page with all the printable worksheets & links found in this book here: www.LivingWellSpendingLess.com/LWSZresources

So are you ready to start your 31 Days of Living Well and Spending Zero challenge?

Let's go!

$\mathcal{D}ay$ 2: **Organize Your Pantry**

I should probably warn you from the start: we are going to be doing a lot of cleaning, organizing, and taking inventory this month! (I never said it was going to be easy!) One of our main goals for the month is to get into the habit of using what we have, rather than buying more. Another goal is to realize and appreciate all that we do have, which is easier to do when our things are cleaned, organized, and inventoried. Sometimes all you need is a fresh look.

> If I had known you were going to put us to work I never would have signed up for this challenge! Just kidding! My pantry is a mess but you make it doable. — Zoey

We will be starting off our challenge for the next few days by planning our food strategy. I don't know about you, but the second I start to think about trying to cook with only the food in my pantry and freezer for a whole month, I start to panic. My brain shuts down, and although my cupboards may in fact be brimming, all I see is "Nothing to eat." Worse, I have found that when I am hungry I make my worst financial decisions. I am willing to spend more when I just want to get food in my belly as quickly as possible!

Our first day of our no-spend, month long challenge involved setting some ground rules and assessing where we were at. Today, we are going to channel that energy and momentum into organizing our pantries.

This particular task might be a little different than pantry cleanups you have done in the past (including in our 31 Days to a Clutter Free Life series http://www.livingwellspendingless.com/clutterfreelife/).

This time, we'll be treating our pantries (and freezers) more like a store. It's time to go through everything, assess what we have on hand, figure out what we need to use up (I'm looking at you, can of beets), and get a general handle on everything.

The first time I posted this guide, several readers posted panicked responses about if it was cheating to buy things like toilet paper, for example. I am in no way advocating that you should start collecting leaves from the backyard! However, this isn't the time to stockpile and hoard either. Yesterday you should have given yourself an allotment for a few needed items. (For example, my family can't go an entire month without bananas, and even the best bunch doesn't last a whole 31 days.)

> My husband and I decided not to buy any food except fruits, veggies, and dairy. After three weeks I had $200 left over. What an awesome feeling.
> — Stacy

When you go through your pantry and freezer, try to think creatively. Think of new ways to use up what you have on hand or ways you can stretch their use. You can make a great pasta dinner with some frozen broccoli, olive oil, and pasta. A big pot of rice, a few cans of corn and beans, and some taco seasoning can make a satisfying Mexican rice bowl that will keep your family sustained for at least a meal or two.

Think simple. And follow these easy steps to bring order to your pantry.

6 Steps to Organize Your Pantry

1. **Clear out a large space to work on.** If you plan to do your cupboards or if your pantry is in your kitchen, you may want to clear off a counter. If your pantry is in another area of the house, like the basement, set up a card table, and be ready to set things out, assess, and put back.

2. **Remove everything from each pantry shelf, one at a time.** Check expiration dates and watch for anything that may have spoiled or is beyond salvaging. Canned items should not be bulging or leaking. Place open items in a cupboard or separate section. I like to keep my unopened items in the pantry, then place items in my cupboards once I've opened them or once they're in use (like baking soda, flour, pasta, and so on).

3. **As you clear each shelf, wipe it down thoroughly.** You can use a multisurface spray, or try a few tablespoons of vinegar diluted in three cups of water. Add a little dish soap and a few drops of your favorite essential oil, and you've got a spray that will freshen and clean without chemicals.

4. **Write down each item as you go.** Use our handy-dandy Pantry Inventory Worksheet to keep track of all your items. This will become your go-to list when you're meal planning. Plus, it'll save you from running back and forth to the pantry for every ingredient.

PANTRY *inventory*

BE SURE TO INDICATE QUANTITY & CROSS ITEMS OFF YOUR LIST AS THEY ARE USED

RICE | POTATOES

VEG | LEGUMES

PASTA

MEAT | TUNA

DRESSINGS

Copyright Living Well Spending Less Inc www.LivingWellSpendingLess.com

Are you surprised to discover items you weren't expecting to find? Didn't realize you had seven cans of corn on hand or an unopened box of cereal that was hiding in the back? Great! Write it down and remember. You may be getting creative with these treasures in the next few weeks.

5. **Put back your pantry items in a clean, logical order.** You're going to want to do it just like the grocery store: each item should be faced towards you, stacked in a way that's easily accessible, and the most popular items should be placed at eye level. If you have several of the same item, check expiration dates and put the oldest item to the front.

6. **Sit back and bask in the beauty of your clean, organized pantry!** Don't you feel calmer now? If you're still feeling ambitious, try tackling the freezer! Use the same process and see what you have stored up.

I did this last night and I was so proud this morning when I opened my pantry and everything was organized. Doing this one day at a time makes it seem possible to spend nothing this month! —Angie

---

FREEZER *inventory*

BE SURE TO INDICATE QUANITY & CROSS ITEMS OFF YOUR LIST AS THEY ARE USED

MEAT & PROTEIN

VEGETABLES

STARCHES

DESSERTS

WHOLE MEALS

BREAKFAST

Copyright © Living Well Spending Less, Inc. www.LivingWellSpendingLess.com

If you've found you're missing a few staples and you know you can't substitute or make it through the month without (or your family might mutiny and boycott the whole process), some folks use this time to pick up these limited items (which you should have allotted for on your worksheet yesterday).

Others like a challenge. If you feel it's better to take an all-or-nothing approach: go for it! Ramen for the month? Hooray! When we did the plan we ate a lot of peanut butter sandwiches, and I was definitely craving something different by the end of the month!

But you know what? We made it through—and I just know you can do it too!

$\mathcal{D}ay$ 3: Plan Your Meals

Welcome to Day 3! Were you at least a little excited this morning when you woke up and thought of your organized pantry and freezer? (Or am I the only one who wakes up excited about organization?)

With a freshly organized freezer and pantry, the load on your shoulders is hopefully just a little bit lighter and you are feeling good about the days to come. When it comes to food, at least now you know what you have; but now you have to figure out how to use it!

Thus, today's assignment is to brainstorm as many meal ideas as possible!

First, as fast as you can, make a list of your family's favorite meals or your favorite recipes. Don't worry if you have the right ingredients; just start writing things down. If your kids are old enough, they can help you with this task. Keep writing until you can't think of any more.

Next, read through your inventory lists and try to think of one dish that corresponds to each different food item. For instance, if canned corn is on your list, you could write down "corn chowder" or "corn casserole" or "goulash." If you are really stumped for an item, keep moving. For items such as ready-to-eat canned soup, it is okay to just jot down "soup."

Print our meal idea worksheet and list your favorite meal ideas from all the brainstorming you've just done. Be sure to cite the source of the recipe. I can't tell you how many times I've gone to make something for a second time and can't find the recipe again (especially online recipes).

Consider your family's tastes. Hopefully the majority of your pantry items fit in with meals your family enjoys. (Otherwise, you may have to really hunker down for a long month.) If there are a few favorite meals, jot them down and assess if you have the ingredients or at least most of the ingredients on hand. Pasta can be substituted for rice or try putting saucy items over toast or baked potatoes if you run out of starches.

Pinterest, Yummly, MyFridgeFood, and other online resources can be really helpful. Check the blogs you follow for recipe ideas as well. There are several lists and recipes at LivingWell Spending-Less.com. To get you started, here is a list of my favorite recipes which can be made from pantry staples.

31 Easy Pantry Staple Recipes:

Get direct links to all 31 recipes at
www.LivingWellSpendingLess.com/LWSZresources

Breakfast
1. Freezer Breakfast Cupcakes
2. Homemade Yogurt
3. Cinnamon Roll Waffles
4. Breakfast Casserole
5. Soups and Chili
6. Taco Soup
7. Beef Stew

8. Corn and Black Bean Chili (vegetarian)
9. Ham and Bean Soup

Sides, Starters, and Snacks
10. Bloomin' Olive Bread
11. Easy Asian Chop Salad
12. Pizza Muffins (vegetarian)
13. Caramel and Cream Cheese Apple Dip
14. No-Fuss Mashed Potatoes
15. Cheesy Potato Casserole

Main Course Meals
16. Grilled Steak Tacos
17. Cheesy Chicken and Rice Casserole
18. Freezer Beef Burritos
19. Slow Cooker Pot Roast
20. Honey Sesame Chicken
21. Spaghetti and Meatball Pie
22. Grandma's Sloppy Joes (optional vegetarian)
23. Easy American Goulash
24. Taco Casserole (optional vegetarian)
25. Taco Bites (optional vegetarian)
26. Easy Pesto Chicken

Dessert
27. One-Bowl Brownies
28. White Chocolate Rice Crispy Treats
29. Five-Minute Ice Cream Cake
30. Maggie and Annie's Everything Cookies
31. Chocolate Insanity Cookies (gluten free)

A few of my favorite dishes are very simple ones, like vegetarian chili made with mostly canned or frozen items; pasta with a simple sauce of olive oil, cracked pepper, and parmesan; or grilled or baked protein with greens or veggies. Sometimes the most satisfying meals are the easiest. Eggs can stretch your meals quite a bit. Try quiche or a frittata and use up the veggies, protein, and condiments you have on hand.

Hopefully your pantry contains some tortillas, bread, rice, grains, or pasta. I find that these items really help round out our meals, plus they can be used in multiple ways. For tortillas, you can make wraps, tacos, quesadillas, pizzas, or even enjoy them with a little cinnamon and sugar as a dessert. Get creative and explore new uses for items you might normally think of as one-trick ponies.

> Yesterday I had finally run out of fresh options and started digging around in the freezer. I found some cooked hamburger and corn. I added them to rice, salsa, seasoning, chicken bouillon, and onions and voila—Hamburger Surprise was born! Pretty good stuff. I did rinse the ice crystals off the meat before I added it to the rice cooker though! Keep those good ideas coming! — Staffanie

I'm a vegetarian, but my family eats meat and I fix it for them pretty regularly. You may find that using a small amount of meat in items like tacos, then adding quinoa or beans, helps to stretch the recipe, while still giving your family a "meaty meal." Mushrooms are another meaty substitute, as are many types of zucchini and squash. Using sausage or bacon (meat with a lot of flavor and oomph) can help make a mostly vegetable meal feel more filled out.

I've had some readers inquire as to how to best create a no-spend meal plan while on a specialty diet. For my family, our pantry and freezer contain items we regularly eat. Hopefully yours does too, and if you follow any specific diet, it should be fine to continue with what you have on hand. If you're gluten-free, you probably have gluten-free pasta or rice flour on hand, and if you're a vegan, you probably have some shelf-stable tofu or almond milk in your storage. Having a month of no spending is no reason to assume you have to eat pasta or cereal at every meal (unless, of course, that's all you had on hand and you're committed to spending absolutely zero).

> If you grow flowers or food, you can trade what you have with a neighbor or at the farmers market.
> ── Jonathan

Another good point raised by readers is that many of us have our own gardens. Now, you may be doing a zero spending month in the winter, or perhaps you have a black thumb and just don't like gardening. However, if you do happen to enjoy gardening, planting and harvesting some staple ingredients like lettuce, herbs, zucchini, or beans can really stretch out your food supply. You don't have to be a farmer to plant a head of lettuce, and you can even grow romaine from the base or "heart" of a used head. Just place in water and put it in a windowsill! How's that for thrifty? You can also try the same process with green onions.

MEAL*ideas*

USE THIS WORKSHEET TO BRAINSTORM MEAL IDEAS TO USE THIS MONTH

MEAL IDEA   FOUND AT

Copyright • Living Well Spending Less Inc www.LivingWellSpendingLess.com

Day 4: Organize a Meal Swap

Now that we've worked on assessing our ingredients and planning out our meals, we have (hopefully) awakened our inner creative chefs and are now practically bursting with meal ideas! This means it is time to do a little proactive meal preparation. The fact is, it is both cheaper and easier to double, triple, or quadruple the same recipe than it is to make four different meals. We are going to take advantage of this fact!

Today your assignment is to call, text, email, or message friends and family and make a plan to swap meals this month.

WANNA swap

WANTED

ONE OR MORE FRIENDS TO PARTICIPATE IN A
WEEKNIGHT MEAL SWAP. YOU COOK ONE
NIGHT, I'LL COOK ANOTHER & WE'LL
BREATHE A LITTLE EASIER

Copyright | Living Well Spending Less, Inc. www.LivingWellSpendingLess.com

Here's how it works: each of you makes multiples of a few easy, freezer-friendly meals, like taco casserole or veggie chili mentioned in Day 3. Send out an APB to your friends and family on Facebook or through email and see who's on board. Usually just a few friends are more than enough to get an exchange going. Be sure to mention any dietary restrictions or other concerns.

> I had a great group of friends who got together to cook each month. We would make forty pizzas, and we each had ten 9" x13" pans for a variety of hot dishes for the freezer. It was awesome. We each came away with four or five pizzas and eight to ten pans ready for slapping into the oven. Great memories. Great food. Great friendships. — *Carol*

Once you've got some friends on board, you just whip up some freezer-friendly meals and swap! You can also agree to deliver meals on a specific day (if freezer meals aren't your thing), or you can even host a meal-making party with friends. Meal swapping is a simple way to save yourself some nights of cooking, mix up your menu a little, and add variety to your meals. You may also end up expanding your repertoire and developing your family's tastes. Who knew your children liked curry? Or maybe you've never been one to cook mushrooms, but your husband loves them. It's exciting to try new dishes while at the same time giving yourself a break in the kitchen.

> I have been doing this for over five years. My parents did it when I was a kid in the seventies. I cook a meal for my family plus two others once a week and deliver it hot to their door at dinnertime. Twice a week, a hot, home-cooked meal arrives at my door at dinnertime ... so that covers three nights. Yes, it is wonderful. — *Heidi*

Consider whether your swap group wants to cook up only main dishes or if you would like to include sides or desserts. It's also nice to stipulate any of your family's dietary preferences or restrictions. The meal swap can be as simple or as complicated as your group sees fit. The idea is to mix things up and have some fun. For more tips and tricks on meal swapping, check out the resources below.

Our group participated in an ingredient swap towards the end of the month long spending freeze because we were all out of that "one" ingredient that would make the meal complete. It was a great way to swap out those canned vegetables or other items that you thought you would use (but didn't) before they expire and go to waste. —Sally

---

11 Meal Swap Resources

Get direct links to all 11 Meal Swap Resources at
www.LivingWellSpendingLess.com/LWSZresources

1. 5 Steps to a Successful Meal Swap (from Real Simple)
2. Organizing Your Freezer Meal Swap (from Frugal Living)
3. How to Set Up a Meal Swap (from Bargain Babe)
4. How to Start a Meal Exchange (from The Simple Dollar)
5. Kitchen Sisters Club (from Beauty and Bedlam)
6. How to Start a Freezer Meal Exchange Club (from Remodelaholic)
7. Freezer Meal Exchange Groups (from Freezer Dinner)
8. Start a Freezer Meal Exchange Group (from Meal Planning Magic)
9. How to Organize a Freezer Meal Swap (from Dollar Store Mom)

10. Start a Meal Exchange Group to Save Money (from Life-hacker)
11. Freezer Meal Swap Sample Guidelines (from Freezer Meal Swap)

If all else fails and you can't find anyone to swap with, try a "family cooking night" or get your husband on board for a "spouse job swap." Offer to do something that he doesn't love to do around the house, and in exchange let him work some kitchen magic. My kids love breakfast for dinner, and sometimes just changing out the order of things can help break up the monotony. Try a savory oatmeal bowl for breakfast or turn leftovers into a breakfast burrito. For lunch, use some dinner leftovers, and then have PB&J for dinnertime!

Mix things up, break out of the rut, and give yourself a break! Spending zero doesn't mean giving up enjoyment of meal times or creating more work for yourself. Get your friends and family on board and get creative!

$\mathcal{D}ay\,5$: Eat 'Out' at Home

Raise your hand if you and your family love going out to eat! My family really loves going to restaurants, so eating out has always been our biggest nonessential expenditure (and money waster!). I know I'm not alone; many of you have shared the very same struggle. Thus, for those of us who enjoy dining out, one of the most difficult parts of the Living Well Spending Zero challenge is resisting that urge to go out to restaurants, order takeout, pick up fast food, run into a coffee shop, or otherwise "treat" yourself with food.

> This is exactly what I needed! We eat out way too much, but if we could copy our favorite meals we could save a lot of money. —Michelle

Honestly, it's not that I even mind cooking. I actually enjoy working in the kitchen. But some nights there's nothing more satisfying than sitting down and being served a meal that someone else cooked.

But here's the good news: You can recreate lots of your favorite fabulous restaurant dishes at home (from appetizers to dinners to desserts)!

You don't have to be much of an Internet sleuth to find out that many chain restaurant recipes taste so good because, well, they aren't exactly health food ... and that's okay sometimes. We don't always have to be perfectly healthy, and sometimes you just need some Olive Garden breadsticks! Still, recreating restaurant recipes at home is not only less expensive, but there's always a chance to sneak in some extra veggies, a little less butter, or to bake instead of fry.

> Making ribs, mac and cheese, grilled veggies, and biscuits, and we're "eating out" at home from everything I already had in the freezer and pantry!
> —Bee

To find your favorite restaurant recipes, there are several websites that specialize in "knockoffs." CopyKat Recipes (http://copykat.com) is a great resource. You can also simply try searching on Yummly and Pinterest. If a local favorite can't be found online, think about the components and get creative.

For instance, a friend of mine is obsessed with the fried pickles at a local restaurant. She couldn't find their recipe online, but after considering what it was about that recipe that she loved, she realized it was the spicy little kick to the batter and the Dijon-mayonnaise dipping sauce. She then found a basic recipe online, kicked up the batter with a little black pepper and cayenne, made a DIY version of the sauce—and voila! She was one happy camper!

You can do it too. Just think about your favorite dish and what makes it so wonderful.

To help you get started, I've included a list of 21 restaurant favorites you can make from home. Check it out and see if your favorite recipe made the list!

21 Restaurant Copycat Recipes

Get direct links to all 21 Copycat Recipes at
www.LivingWellSpendingLess.com/LWSZresources

Starters

1. Homemade Olive Garden Bread Sticks (from Full Bellies, Happy Kids)
2. Chili's Southwest Eggrolls (from CopyKat Recipes)
3. TGI Friday's Baked Potato Skins (from CopyKat Recipes)
4. P.F. Chang's Lettuce Wraps (from Living Well Spending Less)
5. Texas Roadhouse Cinnamon Honey Butter (from Fly Through Our Window)
6. Macaroni Grill Rosemary Bread (from Food.com)
7. Red Lobster Cheddar Bay Biscuits (from ABC News)

Main Courses

8. Outback Steakhouse Alice Springs Chicken (from Fabulously Creative)
9. Panera Broccoli-Cheddar Soup (from Food Network)
10. PF Chang's Mongolian Beef (from Food.com)
11. Applebee's Bourbon Street Steak (from Food.com)
12. Bennigan's Meatloaf (from Cajun Cooking Recipes)
13. Olive Garden Pasta Alfredo (from Budget Savvy Diva)

Sides

14. Chipotle's Cilantro Lime Rice (from Skinnytaste)
15. Cracker Barrel Hashbrown Casserole (from Restaurant Recipes Network)

Desserts

16. Applebee's Walnut Blondie with Maple Butter Sauce (from Just Get Off Your Butt and BAKE)
17. Cheesecake Factory Cheesecake (from Moms Who Think)

Other Treats

18. Starbucks Frappuccinos (from Savory Sweet Life)
19. Cinnabon Cinnamon Rolls (from Beauty and Bedlam)
20. IHOP Cinnastack Pancakes (from Not So Homemade)
21. Starbucks Cranberry Bliss Bars (from Living Well Spending Less)

> On Friday nights we have "fast food home-cooked style"—pizza, tacos/burritos, or burgers! I also make our own bread and rolls, which saves heaps and has none of the nasty additives most store-bought bread has. —Jayne

For today's challenge, try to recreate a restaurant favorite at home! You might be surprised at the amazing savings in food cost alone. Often restaurant recipes cost pennies on the dollar to make. Break out the fancy dishes and cloth napkins if you really want to get the ambiance right, and have a restaurant meal right in the comfort of your own home!

$\mathcal{D}$ay 6: Get in to Freezer Cooking

It's no secret that I am a big fan of freezer cooking, especially easy-to-make "cheater" freezer meals. Not only are they great timesavers, they're also great money savers. Just imagine ... you open your freezer to find an array of delicious options that are all ready to heat up. Unlike typical store-bought convenience meals, you know exactly what's in them. Why? Because you made them yourself!

If you're as busy as I am (which I'm sure you are!), you already know there are some nights when making dinner seems like an insurmountable task. For many of us, that means takeout, fast food, or less-than-healthy options. (Fish sticks and tater tots, anyone?) Freezer meals help you plan ahead and take the stress out of dinner on those busy weeknights.

> It's so hard to find the time for cooking dinner between working from home, changing diapers, and housework. This is going to make meal planning so much easier! —Allison

The other advantage of freezer meals is that you can stretch your ingredients by using them in multiple recipes. Have you ever had a recipe call for half a can of something? What the heck can you do with half a can? Making freezer meals means you can use up the whole can and enjoy your favorite meals whenever you want.

31

Even though we're Living Well and Spending Zero, I always use the following criteria to ensure these meals make the cut.

In my house, each freezer meal must be:

- Deemed delicious by both my kids and my husband (plus additional testers!)
- Require no precooking (aside from browning ground beef)
- Freezer friendly (needless to say!)
- Easy to cook
- Budget friendly: made with inexpensive ingredients and pantry staples (just one reason these recipes are perfect for the Living Well and Spending Zero challenge!)

Freezer Cooking 101

Freezer cooking uses the principle of mass assembly. Your kitchen becomes a production line, where a week's (or even a month's) worth of meals can be created from start to finish and assembled in just an afternoon. In fact, I've come up with several plans that contain go-to foolproof recipes that can be used to create ten freezer meals in about an hour (see recipes below).

If you're new to freezer cooking, you're going to want to take it slow and do a little planning. The good news is you're on a zero spending challenge right now, so most of your "shopping" should come from your own pantry, keeping your costs to the barest minimum. Don't be afraid to substitute ingredients or get creative when necessary!

Go through your list of ingredients from your pantry and freezer (from Day 2) and your list of meal and recipe ideas (from Day 3). Are there a few recipes on your list that can be made ahead and might freeze well? Pick four or five meal ideas to start, and double each recipe so you end up with about ten meals.

> I've got seven kids, and I am right on the brink of my busy season with baseball x2, swim team x2, swimming lessons x2, and marching band x3, all of which happen over the dinner hour. This is the time of year when I stock my freezer with meals. Thanks for getting me off to a great start all in the same place! —Jennifer

Once you have your meal list ready, create a prep sheet and action plan for assembling your recipes. Include cooking instructions and times as well. Be sure your kitchen is ready to go: dishes should be clean and ready to cook. Pots, pans, and counter space should be at the ready.

Always note common ingredients across multiple recipes and prepare them all at once. For example, if several recipes require chopped onions or browned ground beef, take care of all your chopping or browning in one fell swoop. Open all your cans and boxes at the same time, lay out all your ingredients, and go!

Most of the freezer recipes at LivingWellSpendingLess.com are "cheater" recipes—ones that require little to no cooking—so you can just toss all your ingredients in a Ziploc bag, slap on a label, and stick them in the freezer. Mix and match the recipes below or make them all, depending on what you have on hand. To cook, you simply dump your recipe of choice in the crockpot, heat, and eat. It is literally that simple.

If you're still nervous, check out our 7 Easy Tips for Freezer Cooking Like a Pro (http://www.livingwellspendingless.com/2014/02/24/xx-tips-successful-freezer-cooking/). You'll be freezer cooking like it's no sweat in no time!

> I'm reading this, and it's all doable! No fancy ingredients, and yes, these are all pantry items I actually do have in my pantry! —Susie

35 Freezer Meal Ideas

Tackle one set of freezer meals (choose one part to start), or use this list as a jumping-off point for your own freezer meal plan ideas. Each set of five recipes is designed so that you can assemble ten freezer meals in only one hour!

Get direct links to all 7 Freezer Meal Plans at
www.LivingWellSpendingLess.com/LWSZresources

Part 1: The Original
- Honey Lemon Garlic Chicken
- Oh-So-Easy London Broil
- Quick and Easy Taco Soup
- Orange Glazed Pork Chops
- Creamy Italian Chicken

Get the Part 1 Plan Here: http://bit.ly/10Mealsin1Hour

Part 2: Summer Favorites
- Coconut Lime Chicken
- Easy Slow-Cooked Ribs
- Easy Honey Dijon Chicken
- Easy Freezer Pulled Pork
- Hawaiian Chicken

Get the Part 2 Plan Here: http://bit.ly/10MealsinanHour2

Part 3: Easy Comfort Foods
- Grandma's Sloppy Joes
- Herb Roasted Chicken Breast
- Easy Slow Cooker Pot Roast

- Easy Tomato Parmesan Chicken
- Slow Cooked Pork Tenderloin

Get the Part 3 Plan Here: http://bit.ly/10MealsinOneHour3

Part 4: Easy Winter Classics
- Cheesy Chicken and Rice Casserole
- Easy Freezer Ham and Bean Soup
- Simple Cranberry Chicken
- Balsamic Roast Beef
- Sweet and Spicy Chinese Chicken

Get the Part 4 Plan Here: http://bit.ly/10MealsinOneHour4

Part 5: Flavorful Favorites
- Freezer-to-Crockpot Chicken Fajitas
- Crockpot Beef Burritos
- Kale and White Bean Soup with Sausage
- Creamy Mushroom Pork Chops
- Honey Sesame Chicken

Get the Part 5 Plan Here: http://bit.ly/10MealsinOneHour5

Part 6: Global Flavors
- Easy Thai Chicken
- Easy Pesto Chicken
- Grilled Steak Tacos
- Easy Greek Chicken
- Easy Freezer Bacon and Blue Cheese Burgers

Get the Part 6 Plan Here: http://bit.ly/10MealsinOneHour6

Part 7: Fresh Flavors

- Simple Summer Chicken Sandwich
- Spice Rubbed Steak Salad
- Easy Chicken Satay
- White Bean Chili
- Easy Crockpot Lettuce Wraps

Get the Part 7 Plan Here: http://bit.ly/10MealsinOneHour7

Again, be sure to consider what you have on hand when you create your freezer meal menu for today's challenge. If you have meat on hand, try a few of my meat recipes.

> Love these recipes and you give great steps to make it easier to follow along. Freezer meals have become a staple in my household, and I love finding new recipes. —Suzanne

Freezer cooking is a great way to save money, time, and sanity. After today's challenge, you'll feel like you have a handle on what to eat for the month, and you'll know exactly how to use up all those pantry ingredients you just discovered on Day 1. Freezer meals help you stretch your staples and keep your family happy and full!

$\mathcal{D}ay\,7$: Reflection

You've already made it an entire week! Can you believe it? What was the biggest challenge for you? What was the biggest lesson you learned?

> The first week was actually pretty good. I am so impressed with how much my hubby is on board! We've not eaten out at all, which is the biggest adjustment, but I'm excited because it's so much healthier for us too. It's amazing how much you really don't need to buy things! —*Leslie*

The very first time my own family took on a spending freeze challenge, I have to admit that I questioned my sanity a little bit. I wondered if I was depriving my children, and I couldn't help but question whether I would actually be able to make it an entire month. I may have even had a mini-crisis of sorts.

Being on a spending freeze is hard. Sometimes you feel like it's too restrictive—or just plain nutty, especially when your friends or family members question it, laugh at you, or try to break your resolve with temptations. After all, while many of us need to scale back our mindless spending a little, most of us don't need a complete moratorium.

Wow, what a week! Instead of organizing the pantry, I decided to paint it and cover the shelves too. After a lot of frustration, anger, and tears came a complete meltdown. However, after a good night's sleep and a new perspective, I now have a beautiful, organized pantry and freezer that makes me happy and calmer. I am already feeling more in control and less anxious! —Sue

The fact is, this challenge is a little extreme, and that's okay. Sometimes we need a little extreme in our lives to gain a deeper appreciation for what we do have, while enjoying the little blessings and small moments in life. Going a month without spending is definitely a growth experience.

This has been a crazy week! On the flip side, I am realizing how blessed we are. We spent the whole day with family and brought dinner for everyone from our stockpile; it was one of the most beautiful, relaxing days we've all had in a while. It truly is causing me to focus more on my blessings and my family. —Sam

When we did our first challenge, we suffered through a pretty "empty" pantry—one that seemed to be full of condiments and really, not much else. A few days in, I overheard my oldest explain to her sister how we couldn't purchase candy, because candy was "a want, not a need."

A day or two later, I picked them up from a playdate, during which they'd been treated to McDonald's. The mom of their friend observed that she had never before seen two kids so excited about a Happy Meal.

For a moment, under the scrutiny of another mom questioning my judgment, I starting feeling guilty, like the "weirdo" mom that was forcing them into this spending freeze.

But suddenly it clicked and I had my aha moment for the week: my girls were learning the exact lessons I was hoping they would! They'd gained an understanding of the difference between a want and a need. They'd gained a deeper appreciation for little treats like McDonald's Happy Meals, and they were grateful rather than just blowing things off as the norm.

As uncomfortable as it may have been, I realized that Week 1— with all of its bumps and snags and strange pasta dishes—was a success! We were pulling together as a family while learning to appreciate what we already had.

> Today I completely broke down trying to make my careful "essentials only" grocery list. After being interrupted by my little angels for the 100th time in a twenty-minute period, I looked right at my husband and told him to take the children to McDonald's. So yes, I caved. Now I am back on track. I loved that your girls caught on to this. I need to involve my children more, and it's a good reminder! —Claire

Time for Reflection

And now's the time for your reflections on the week. Take a few moments today and write down your observations. What's been the biggest challenge in spending nothing? What surprised you? What would you do differently next time or in the future?

You may also want to ponder for a minute on the state of your finances. How much have you saved this week, compared to similar weeks in the past? Give yourself kudos if you managed to refrain from that fancy coffee drink or pass up a trip to the store.

Did you find new modes of entertainment for your family? Were there any epiphanies? Any funny moments?

Day 7: Reflection

If I feel the "want" to shop, I always feel good that I get a lot for a little by shopping at the Dollar Tree. Well, I literally had a mini panic attack as I drove by the Dollar Tree on my way home from work today ... I could justify "needing" something in there. Well, I didn't stop! I didn't shop! I made it home, and I finally relaxed. All is well in the world and I didn't spend a dollar today at Dollar Tree.

P.S. My largest one-time purchase at Dollar Tree? Sit down ... $405.00! —*Jacqueline*

Whatever lessons you take away from this week, now's the time to write them down and keep track. Be honest with yourself about your successes and struggles.

I've even included a pretty worksheet to help you document your journey!

WEEKLY *reflection*

■ **What was the SCARIEST part of starting this challenge?**

goals FOR NEXT WEEK

■ **What is the ONE thing you are most excited to get out of this challenge?**

■

■ **What has been the BIGGEST struggle this week?**

■

■ **Where were you most tempted (or where did you) CHEAT?**

■ **Did you have any "AHA!" moments?**

■ **What are you MOST worried about looking forward?**

■ **What has been the MOST surprising thing about not spending this week?**

We're about to delve into Week 2. Congratulations!

41

week
TWO

clean &
ORGANIZE

Day 8: Get Ready to Clean

Welcome to Week 2!

Last week, we talked a lot about food and organizing what we eat. We discussed some ideas for freezer meals and for making restaurant meals at home. The purpose of our focus on food was due to the fact that we all make poor financial decisions when we're hungry!

But other pitfalls can trip us up too. We let our homes get chaotic and cluttered and dirty and then foolishly think spending money is going to fix the problem. We buy ourselves new mops or cleaners or organizers, thinking they will make the mess waiting at home magically disappear. Sometimes we simply can't stand the thought of being trapped in the chaos so we choose going out—and spending money—over staying in.

This week we're going to roll up our sleeves and get the rest of the house in order! How many of us have purchased an item (batteries, candles, lightbulbs, toiletries, crafts, office supplies, etc.) only to come home and realize that we had that exact item stashed away somewhere and just forgot about it? I once realized I had eight tubes of super glue. Eight! We also seem to have that problem with ChapStick. (And yet, somehow I still can never seem to find a tube when I need some. What's up with that?)

This week we are going to tackle the chaos head on. We are going to scrub and dust and sort and purge and really, truly get our spaces clean. It doesn't matter who you are or where you live, whether you own or rent, have a professionally decorated home or a jumble of mismatched secondhand furniture: you will like your house better—and enjoy being home more—when it is clean.

There is no better way to truly appreciate what you have than to take care of it. If you're feeling like your house is a little shabby or your clothes are a little worn, then this is the perfect time to spruce things up. Cleaning and refreshing a few items around the house will give them new life and provide you with a sense of accomplishment.

But don't worry, we are going to take it slow. In fact, today your assignment is to simply get ready to clean. We are going to do a few things today that will make your big cleaning day easier, plus give you some time to get into the "gotta clean" mindset. By tomorrow you will be raring to go, I promise. Well, okay, maybe not raring to go, per se, but at the very least, resigned to the idea. And because I'm nice like that, I've even created a cute checklist to help you get ready. Now if that's not motivation, I don't know what is!

Buying/organizing/cleaning/decorating when the house is a mess is a mistake I make a lot! I spent several hours today organizing things and getting ready for cleaning day tomorrow, and the house already looks awesome—way better than it does most of the time. It's exciting! —Jenny

CLEANING PREP
checklist

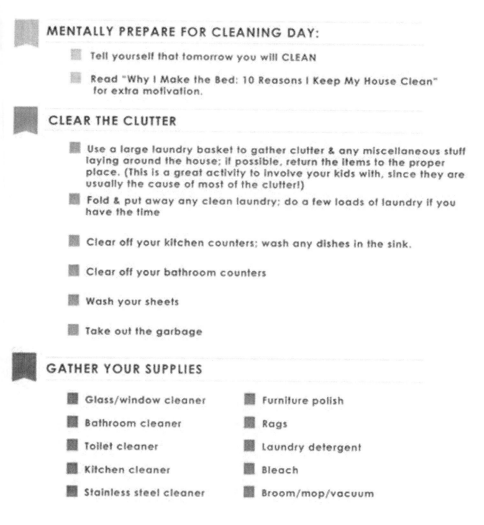

MENTALLY PREPARE FOR CLEANING DAY:

- [ ] Tell yourself that tomorrow you will CLEAN

- [ ] Read "Why I Make the Bed: 10 Reasons I Keep My House Clean" for extra motivation.

CLEAR THE CLUTTER

- [ ] Use a large laundry basket to gather clutter & any miscellaneous stuff laying around the house; if possible, return the items to the proper place. (This is a great activity to involve your kids with, since they are usually the cause of most of the clutter!)

- [ ] Fold & put away any clean laundry; do a few loads of laundry if you have the time

- [ ] Clear off your kitchen counters; wash any dishes in the sink.

- [ ] Clear off your bathroom counters

- [ ] Wash your sheets

- [ ] Take out the garbage

GATHER YOUR SUPPLIES

- [ ] Glass/window cleaner
- [ ] Bathroom cleaner
- [ ] Toilet cleaner
- [ ] Kitchen cleaner
- [ ] Stainless steel cleaner

- [ ] Furniture polish
- [ ] Rags
- [ ] Laundry detergent
- [ ] Bleach
- [ ] Broom/mop/vacuum

Copyright © Living Well Spending Less, Inc. www.LivingWellSpendingLess.com

Planning Ahead

The first thing you have to do today is tell yourself that tomorrow, no matter what, you are going to clean your house. Repeat it to yourself all day long.

If you need some inspiration, I highly recommend reading this post on "Why I Make the Bed: 10 Reasons I Keep My House Clean" (http://www.livingwellspendingless.com/2012/02/15/why-i-make-my-bed-10-reasons-i-keep-my-house-clean/) or this post on "Speed Cleaning" (http://www.livingwellspendingless.com/2010/09/08/speed-cleaning/). While you work on your cleaning list, think about the areas in your home that are probably going to need some extra attention.

The next thing you're going to want to do is take a few minutes to plan and assemble. Keep reminding yourself that tomorrow is going to be your day to clean! Mental preparation is key!

Take a few minutes to do some picking up. Set the timer for fifteen, thirty, or sixty minutes—the more time you can spare, the better—and make your way around the house, picking up the obvious clutter. I like to use a laundry basket—it's easy to carry—and just gather up any shoes, coats, bags, or toys that are lying around.

If you're a little behind on cleaning, get the dishes out of the sink and run a few loads of laundry. Clear and stash any cosmetics lying around in the bathroom, and clear out all that clutter that collects on your kitchen counters or in your entryway. The idea is to get things squared away so you can start the real cleaning tomorrow.

Finally, assemble your cleaning supplies. Are you out of anything? Freeze! Do not run to the store! There's probably a substitute right in your own cupboard.

Check out our list of 10 Green and Thrifty Cleaning Products you can make right at home using just ten basic ingredients (http://www.livingwellspendingless.com/2013/03/13/green-thrifty-cleaning-products/). Chances are you probably have everything you need already on hand!

> I did a deep clean of my kitchen this weekend, and I'm amazed at how removing chaos has improved my mood. Thanks for reminding me that I can feel the same about the entire house. The cute checklist and a day to mentally prepare helped too! —Angie

For more ideas on cleaners and inspiration, you may want to check out Martha Stewart online, Real Simple, and Better Homes and Gardens, which all have plenty of great cleaning resources.

Now get a good night's rest, because tomorrow we clean!

> It's so weird to me that I'm so excited to be cleaning my house, but it's true! I think that knowing that I'm not alone in doing this task makes it the most fun! Looking forward to tomorrow's challenge. It's really lighting the fire to get my home life more together! —Sam

Day 9: Clean Your House

We've arrived! It's cleaning day! I know you're as excited as I am! Can I get a little woot woot?

The older I get, the more of a clean freak I become. But I wasn't always that way, and even now, keeping things neat and tidy certainly does not come naturally to me. It is still something I have to work at every single day. It is still something I have to gear up to do. It is still work.

To me, cleaning my house is worth the effort. I spend a lot of time at home, probably more than most people. I am more productive, more peaceful, more creative, more engaged, more fun when my house is clean. I enjoy my life and space so much more when it is tidy. So I clean. And today, so will you.

And as silly as it sounds, I truly do get excited about cleaning. It's a chance to have a fresh start, to put everything to rest, and to feel like you're in control of your domain. Spending some time working from home, I've gained a strong appreciation for all of the things your home can be: your office, your rest space, your sanctuary, and your social space, all in one. Keeping it clean, organized, and beautiful is important to all aspects of your life.

In fact, your home should be your retreat: the space you find most welcoming and restful. It shouldn't be a place of chaos, but a place of respite.

For those of you who are worried about trying to deep clean your whole house in one day, stop! We are going to tackle a big chunk of it today, but not quite all of it. There will be selective areas that we ignore until later. But our bathrooms will sparkle, our countertops will shine, and our main living areas will be clean.

So let's get started!

> Woot! Cleaning is totally my favorite thing to do. With my husband and two children it is sometimes difficult. My goal is to get a whole lot more organized. The checklists are very helpful, so thank you and God bless! —Yvette

My personal strategy is to start with the room I dread cleaning the most: the bathroom. I then do the kitchen, since that is my next least favorite, and from there work my way through the rest of the house. After I've cleaned the bathroom and the kitchen, made the beds, and picked up any clutter (I throw it all in a basket for the kids to help put away), I find it more efficient to do things like dusting, window cleaning, vacuuming, and mopping throughout the whole house all at once, not room by room.

I've prepared another checklist for you to use while you clean today. You'll notice that there are a few things conspicuously missing, such as the home office, the closets, and the kids' rooms. This is intentional. We will get there! For today, just focus on the main living areas, the bathrooms, and your own bedroom.

Take a few moments to review the checklist below, and please feel free to adapt it to fit your home, as I know not all of us have a dining room or a basement or a family room. The idea here is to clean as much of your main living space as you can today.

CLEANING DAY
checklist

CLEAN YOUR KITCHEN

Unload/load the dishwasher

Wash, dry, & put away any non-dishwasher items

Wipe down appliances

Clean & sanitize countertops; wipe dry with clean towel

Clean sink; wipe dry

Sweep & mop floor

CLEAN YOUR DINING ROOM

Wipe down table & chairs

Polish table (if wood)

Sweep/vacuum

CLEAN YOUR BATHROOM(S)

Clean toilet

Scrub tub/shower; wipe dry with clean rag

Scrub sink & countertop; wipe dry with clean rag

Clean mirror(s)

Sweep & mop floor

CLEAN YOUR BEDROOM(S)

Make the bed

Pick up & put away clothes, shoes, etc.

Clear off & dust dresser(s)

Sweep/vacuum

CLEAN YOUR LIVING AREA(S)

Dust tables & shelves

Fluff throw pillows

Pick up anything that is out of place

Sweep/vacuum

DEEP cleaning TASKS

Clean windows & mirrors

Dust ceiling fans

Clean baseboards

Dust/vacumm under furniture

Swwep or vacuum all floors

Wash throw rugs

 . . . Living Well Spending Less Inc www.LivingWellSpendingLess.com

> I am a neat freak who struggles to keep things tidy! But I have two toddlers, so I've made my peace with it for now. Gotta go ... time to clean! — Alisha

At the end of the day your countertops should sparkle! Your floors should glisten! Your couch cushions should be fluffed and in their proper place!

Today is the day, so without further ado, let's get cleaning!

> I'm looking forward to this challenge ... or rather, I'm looking forward to the end of the day when the challenge is complete! —Carrie

Day 10: Clean Your Kids' Rooms

Before we go on, I want to add a little word of advice. It seems as though at this point in the challenge people sometimes start becoming overwhelmed. So let me just reassure you that it's going to be okay! I promise.

Cleaning the house can be a rewarding and wonderful way to get a handle on what you have and to keep you cognizant of the many blessings in your life. Mentally, it marks a fresh start and adds a tangible way to show that you're committing to a new lifestyle and gaining control over spending and excess (the very reason for starting our zero-spend challenge).

However, if it takes longer than one day to clean your house or if life just gets in the way, please, please, please don't abandon the challenge! The real objective is to spend 31 Days of Spending Zero. The rest is to simply help you on the way. So if your house isn't 100 percent clean at this point, don't beat yourself up. Keep going and move forward. Look at how far you've come in just ten days! We're nearly one-third of the way through the challenge, and you're doing great!

So Let's Keep Going!

Today we're going to get a handle on the room or rooms occupied by some of our biggest mess makers ... our kiddos. I don't know about the rest of you, but if it weren't for my darling children, my house would be clean all the time. Okay, maybe not all the time, but almost all the time. How can two such seemingly sweet and innocent girls be such incredible mess makers? I'm betting your kids are the same way.

Some of you may be familiar with that now infamous post "Why I Took My Kids' Toys Away"(http://www.livingwellspendingless. com/toys). It has been a few years since I first wrote that post, and while I'd love to report that my kids' room is never a mess ... I'd be lying.

We still struggle with keeping things in check, separating needs from wants, and cutting back on excess. We've grown leaps and bounds since "the great purge," but we still have to take the time to clean and organize regularly.

And so today, together, we conquer the kids' rooms. If your kids are old enough to help, today is also the day to enlist their help and get them on board with the challenge. Cleaning their room together with you offers a great opportunity for feedback and learning, as they take an active role in your new family lifestyle. You may also learn a few things about what's important to them.

I did it today! How exciting! Well, maybe exciting is the wrong word. Liberating is a better word. I have three girls and three bedrooms. It took me a total of six hours. I got a thirty-gallon bag of garbage and a thirty-gallon bag of donations from each girl's room, plus two bags of hand-me-downs for my nieces. That's a lot of stuff I no longer have to wade through and sort and put away again! Thank you for the motivation! —Hillary

---

kids ROOM CLEANING checklist

KIDS ROOM CLEANING

- Make the bed
- Sort clothes into 4 piles
- **SORT ANYTHING THAT:**
  - Is too small that you would like to keep for a sibling
    Place in a hand-me-down box clearly marked with the correct sizes
  - Is out of season that will still fit next year
    Place in a seasonal box i.e. "summer clothing" box
  - No longer fits but you would like to keep as a "keepsake:
    Place in a keepsake box
- **GIVE ANYTHING THAT:**
  - No longer fits
  - There is no one to hand it down to
  - Is in good condition
  - Your child refuses to wear
- **KEEP ANYTHING THAT:**
  - Still fits
  - Is seasonally appropriate
  - Is in good condition
- **TOSS ANYTHING THAT:**
  - Is badly stained, frayed, or torn

TOYS

- **SORT ANYTHING THAT:**
  - Is not currently played with but might be used later or you want to keep for a sibling
  - Has any sort of sentimental value
- **GIVE ANYTHING THAT:**
  - Is no longer played with
  - You are sick of picking up the pieces
  - Doesn't fit within your "keep" criteria
- **KEEP ANYTHING THAT:**
  - Encourages imaginative play or is educational
  - Is played with frequently
- **TOSS ANYTHING THAT:**
  - That is broken.

DEEP cleaning TASKS

- Re-organize drawers & closet
- Label everything!
- Dust & wipe down surfaces
- Clean windows/mirrors
- Sweep or vacuum all floors

Copyright © Living Well Spending Less, Inc. www.LivingWellSpendingLess.com

I've included the above checklist as a guide, but please feel free to modify it to suit your own needs. I do recommend that you start by making the bed, and then work on tackling the stuff.

Beginning with clothing, sort all the items into four piles—Store, Give, Keep, and Toss. Then tackle the toys and do the same. Once you've sorted your items, it's time to organize them into the drawers and closet. Label storage as you go, and dust and clean all the now-cleared-off surfaces. Finish off the room with a good wipe down of all mirrors, windows, and touch points, and vacuum the floors.

The sorting is the toughest part, so once you've got a handle on that, the rest is easy-peasy. Resist the urge to run out and purchase storage containers, boxes, and bags. Instead, make do with what you have on hand. (We're spending zero, remember?) Consider items that can be traded for things you might need (save them for Day 25), sold on eBay or Craigslist (save them for Day 22), or handed down to someone else. Don't be afraid to get creative!

My girls donated many of their old toys and games to our church nursery, where they could "revisit" the items occasionally and see them put to good use. They were even proud to give their items away and share them with their friends!

My husband and I take at least one full day about every two to three months to sit down with each one of our children to help them clean and purge items. Between clothes, shoes, toys, and school items, they each usually donate two bags of items and one bag of garbage. I have found that by doing this regularly, my children are very good at deciding for themselves what toys they do not play with anymore and are more than happy to give to another child. I believe this will help them in the long run to not want or even purchase items that they do not need. —Stacie

For some reason, kids' rooms can feel like the literal eye of the storm, so once that area is tamed, you might be amazed at how much better life becomes. Suddenly entertainment is easier to come by (you'll rediscover all those books and games that were forgotten!), and your children will learn important lessons about appreciating what they have on hand.

For more inspiration, visit my one-year follow-up post to Why I Took My Kids' Toys Away (http://www.livingwellspendingless. com/2013/09/13/why-i-took-my-kids-toys-away-one-year-later/).

$\mathcal{D}ay$ 11: Organize Your Office

It's now the middle of Week 2 and one-third of the way through our challenge, and by now you should be feeling pretty good about all you've achieved so far—your meals are organized and you have a handle on your food, your living areas and kids' rooms are clean, and things are coming right along.

Best of all you've been saving money—you've managed to achieve all of this without spending a dime! Don't forget to take the time to pat yourself on the back. You're doing great!

Organize Your Family Command Center

Today it's time to get a handle on our paperwork. Many of us have a home office area or a central "hub." This Family Command Center is an essential place where we store bills, paperwork, cards, and more. If you're a crafter, this might be your studio. If you work from home, you probably consider this area your office. Whether it's a corner in your kitchen or an entire room, all of us have some place where we stash all our important paperwork. And if you don't have one, you probably need one.

Today is the day we revamp that critical space and get back in control!

I try to keep my home neat and tidy most of the time, but this is definitely one area where I struggle. The daily tasks are so motivating! —*Susan*

Whenever I tackle my desk, I'm always sort of amazed. As hard as I try to stay on top of it (and these days, I really do, for the most part), I always manage to find at least something that I've forgotten. It might be a gift card, a bill, a thank-you card that I haven't mailed ... something. Whatever it is, I always walk away from the desk feeling like I've been on a bit of a treasure hunt. (Okay, maybe not when I find a forgotten bill, but it could be worse.)

Oh, my goodness, my desk is such a disaster area, and my inbox looks like a "Before" picture. I always think that I should do something about it, and then it just seems too overwhelming so I put it off another day. I love the checklists—they make it so manageable! Thanks again, Ruth! —*Denise*

For today's challenge, I've created another printable list (below) to help you plan and keep you on task. Before you start, you're going to want to get out a trash bin, a recycle bin, and a shredder, in addition to a few boxes or bins to help you get organized.

home OFFICE CLEANING checklist

GET OUT A GARBAGE CAN, RECYCLE BIN, & SHREDDER

HOME OFFICE CLEANING

CLEAR YOUR DESK:
- Put paperwork in a pile to sort in a bit
- Return anything that doesn't belong to other room

EMPTY YOUR DESK DRAWERS:
- Put like items together
- Add any paperwork & receipts to the to-sort pile
- Return anything that doesn't belong to other rooms
- Toss any broken items in the garbage

RE-ORGANIZE YOUR DESK DRAWERS:
- If your drawers do not have dividers, be sure to find one or create one out of supplies you have around the house
  - I used cigar boxes, which you can often get free from the local cigar shop!
- Put like items together & limit drawer items to things you use regularly & need to have close at hand

ORGANIZE WRITING UTENSILS:
- Quickly test all pens, pencils, & highlighters & toss any that no longer work
- Use a pretty cup/pencil holder to store them

SORT THROUGH PAPERWORK & INBOX:
- File anything that is essential to record-keeping or that you will need to reference in the future
- Toss or recycle anything that is no longer relevant or you will not need in the future
- Pay bills or prepare them for payment
- Gather all post-its, notes, or flyers & add them to one master to-do list or calendar
- Recycle any outdated letterhead, business cards, etc.

DEEP cleaning TASKS

- Clean & polish your desk
- Organize your cords
- Organize any cabinets
- Organize & dust shelfs & surfaces
- Sweep or vacuum

Copyright © Living Well Spending Less, Inc. www.LivingWellSpendingLess.com

Don't be afraid to get creative! The first time I did this challenge, I found a whole stack of cigar boxes in the garage that were left over from our cigar-themed wedding (cigar stores will often give these away for free), and I ended up using them as drawer organizers. They worked perfectly, and I still use them to this day! You could also cover a can or shoebox with some pretty paint or washi tape. It really is amazing how innovative we can be when forced to improvise!

A home office doesn't need to be expensive, but since we're spending nothing right now, simply use what you have on hand and repurpose items as you go!

I like to use food boxes to organize my drawers. I usually go to my pantry and see what's about empty and cut the boxes to fit in the drawer. Cheez-its, fruit snacks, granola bars ... those boxes fit perfectly with no need to go out and buy something new or waste the gas going to a store to ask for free boxes!

—Jen

After that, it's just a matter of sorting papers and organizing drawers. Empty all the drawers and wipe out the nooks and crannies. Organize your cords and wipe down your keyboard and tools to keep them free of crumbs and dust. Toss out anything that's outdated or past its prime. I tend to keep clippings from articles and things I intend to read, but if they're over a month old, file or recycle! Test out your pencils and pens and keep the items that work and are clean. Toss anything that's leaky, broken, or no longer useful.

Once you're organized, simply dust and vacuum the space and wipe off handles and surfaces.

And now you're all set and ready to tackle anything that comes across your work surface! Don't you feel motivated?

$\mathcal{D}ay$ 12: **Organize Your Closet**

Day 12! We're almost through Week 2, and if you've been keeping up, you should be feeling a little more orderly and in control of your space.

Before we dive into today's task, let me recommend that you take a little time to speed clean each day. (You can find the post and checklist here: http://www.livingwellspendingless. com/2010/09/08/speed-cleaning/.) This will help you maintain momentum and feel in control of your space. Taking just a few minutes each day to tidy the house will help you continue with the good habits you've established during the course of the challenge.

And while we're on a path to changing our mentality and our daily lives, you may also want to take this opportunity to start adopting some new good habits that can change your life for the better. Get tips and ideas for forming new habits here: http:// www.livingwellspendingless.com/2015/03/27/10-good-habits-will-change-life/.

So guess what? Today, to reward ourselves for all our hard work, we're going to go shopping!

Wait—what?

Not real shopping, silly! We're on a zero-spending challenge, remember? But that doesn't mean we can't reward ourselves with a chance to look fabulous. It's time to dive into what we have and get creative. Let's see what we can spruce up and simplify.

Shop Your Closet

If you're anything like me, you have a closet full of clothes—and yet you always feel like you have nothing to wear. Every outfit feels like you're just one accessory or one blouse away from getting that "perfect" look. You probably have a pair or two of jeans that don't quite fit since you had your last baby, or a few shirts that still have the tags on them that you bought because they were such a great deal, but either didn't fit quite right from the get-go, didn't go with anything else you owned, or didn't really fit your tastes.

Today it's time to get a handle on this stuff! So often we buy clothing, shoes, and accessories to fill some sort of void. (And yes, I am talking about myself.) We feel like we need or deserve a treat, so we think this one "little" item will make all the difference for us.

Most of us, however, have almost everything we need, and it's already in our possession. Sometimes, when we take a moment to get a handle on what we have, we discover that we don't need anything new!

The 40 Hanger Closet

A few years ago, on a whim, I pared my jam-packed, overstuffed closet to just forty hangers (http://www.livingwellspendingless.com/2013/05/24/40-hanger-closet/).

For me, this was a pretty drastic approach to organizing my wardrobe, but it also made a dramatic difference in both my attitude and my sanity. Although I got rid of three quarters of my clothes, my wardrobe actually felt much bigger!

Now, in my approach, one of the steps is to yes, go out and buy some really nice hangers. (I recommend hangers with velvet coating to keep your clothes from slipping off.) But you know what? For now you're going to make do with the hangers you already have on hand. You probably have plenty.

The advantage of the 40 Hanger Closet (or 35 or 50, whatever works best for you) is that it gives you a finite framework. You have to examine each piece of clothing in your closet under the context of:

- Do I love it?
- Does it fit?
- Is it in good condition?

If it doesn't fit all three criteria, it doesn't make the cut.

Never again will you walk into your closet and proclaim, "I have nothing to wear!" You'll love and want to wear everything in your wardrobe. In the time since, I have maintained this 40-hanger philosophy, and it just makes life so much simpler! I haven't regretted it once. I actually feel like I have much more to wear, and I love everything I own. If I find an item to buy, I have to really love it to kick out a resident member of my closet—because for every item that goes in, one item goes out. And because I already like what I have, that also makes me much more picky about what comes in!

I gave myself three hours yesterday to work on your 40 hanger suggestion. While I didn't get that far, I did try on every piece of clothing in my closet. I laughed, I cried, I put items in piles for consignment, and though I still have way too much, it felt good to know that everything there fits—a lot of it didn't! In the end I came out with 97 empty hangers! — Jacqueline

The other advantage is that I can find everything! It's organized by color, and I can quickly see where my brown sweater or my green button-down is. I'm no longer rushed before going some-where because I'm searching for a belt or a pair of shoes to match, plus my clothes stay wrinkle-free and neat because they aren't crammed into a closet or falling on the floor.

Organizing Your Closet

Here's my handy printable checklist to follow as you start to or-ganize your closet.

bedroom CLOSET CLEANING checklist

BEFORE STARTING YOUR CLOSET, MAKE YOUR BED & TIDY UP THE REST OF YOUR ROOM

WEED FIRST

Take out the following items & place them on the bed:
- Any items you haven't worn or used in a year
- Any items you don't like
- Any clothing that doesn't fit
- Any items that are ripped, stained, or unwearable
- Any items that are out of season

SORT ITEMS INTO 3 PILES

GOODWILL PILE: For items to donate (only donate good condition items)
SELL PILE: For higher value items such as purses or designer clothing
TOSS PILE: For damaged items
BOX OR BAG DONATION & STORAGE ITEMS: Place a dryer sheet in the box
keep items fresh, & take care of the toss pile. Set the "Sell" pile aside for now.

CLEAR THE CLOSET

EMPTY THE CLOSET:
- Lay all the clothes on the bed; make sure they are all hung correctly,
facing the same direction on sturdy hangers. Toss any broken hangers.
- Place shoes, purses, & other accessories in piles of like item.
- Add to the Goodwill, Sell, Store, or Toss piles as needed
- Assess the empty space. You have to put things back
the way they were--consider different options
- CLEAN the empty space--dust shelves (even wire ones);
sweep or vacuum the floor

PUT IT ALL AWAY

DEEP cleaning TASKS

PUT THINGS BACK:
- Re-hang clothing in a way that makes sense
* I like to sort items by category & color
- Replace shoes, sorting them by type & color
- Pay bills or prepare them for payment
- Gather all post-its, notes, or flyers & add
them to one master to-do list or calendar
- Recycle any outdated letterhead, business cards, etc.

- Sort clothes every few months
- Re-organize often
- Toss worn & torn items often
- Toss broken hangers often

Copyright · Living Well Spending Less, Inc. www.LivingWellSpendingLess.com

Before you begin, take a few moments to spruce up your bedroom and make sure your work surface is clean. Make your bed and pick up items that are near the closet.

First you're going to weed through the items that are currently in your closet. Pull out anything that doesn't fit, that you don't like, or that you haven't worn in a year. Remove items that are ripped, stained, or unwearable. These items will be sorted into three categories—Goodwill/Sell, Toss, and Store for Later. Items that are specifically seasonal (your bathing suit in Minnesota or turtleneck sweaters in Texas) may need to be stored. My husband convinced me to store some items that I wasn't sure about purging. Revisit them in six months and it will be a much easier decision.

Now look through the remaining items and repeat the process one more time.

Make sure every item fits, is in good shape, and is loved.

Now, remove the items from your closet. Since you might not be upgrading your hangers this month, simply assess the hangers you have and toss anything that's broken. Count out the number of items you have remaining and make sure there are only 40 (or keep purging). I also like to set a number for shoes and handbags or accessories and stay within that number.

Assess your empty closet space—clean it, vacuum it, and get rid of any dust bunnies or dirt. If there are any items that belong elsewhere, it's time to move them to their home. Rehang your clothing and sort by category or color, whatever makes sense to you. Replace your shoes, organizing them in a shoe rack or in boxes. Try stuffing your boots with rolled-up magazines to help them hold their shape. Add in your accessories, purses, bags, and other items, then bask in the splendor of your organized closet!

Trust me, you're not the only one who just loves to stare at a freshly organized closet. I always leave my closet door open nonstop for a couple of days after I clean just to look at it! —*Sophia*

10 Free Ways to Organize Your Closet

Get direct links to all 10 Closet Organizing Ideas at www.LivingWellSpendingLess.com/LWSZresources

1. Crown Molding Shoe Rack (from Picklee)
2. DIY Scarf Holder (from Snapguide)
3. Towel Wrack Scarf Solution (from Apartment Therapy)
4. Painted Crate Shoe Holder (from Thea's Mania)
5. Wooden Hanger Belt Rack (from Martha Stewart)
6. Shoebox Drawer Dividers (from Yahoo)
7. Cardboard Drawer Dividers (from A Real Housewife of NYC)
8. Cluster Organization (from HGTV)
9. Paper-Lined Storage Bins (from Organizing Made Fun)
10. Hanging Flip Flop Holders (from EPBOT)

10 FREE
WAYS to
ORGANIZE
your CLOSET

$\mathcal{D}ay$ 13: Organize Your Bathroom

Bathrooms are funny places, aren't they? The room where you get all nice and clean can somehow end up being the most disorganized wreck of a room in the entire house! And I'm not talking about all the yucky scrubbing-the-toilet and soap scum stuff. (Hopefully you tackled that a few days ago when you cleaned and now you're maintaining it by speed cleaning each day!)

> I know the bathroom is the easiest in the house to ignore, but I love when it's nice and organized!
> —Janett

No, what I really take issue with is not the cleaning, it's the keeping it organized. It is figuring out what to do with all those "bottles of crap," as my husband so lovingly refers to them, all the makeup and tubes of cream, all the hairspray and curling irons and flat irons (oh my!). It's the pile of towels and the extra toilet paper and the set of rollers that I've only used twice and the piles and piles and piles of ponytail holders and barrettes that seem to multiply while I sleep, and all those mini-samples from your last seven hotel stays.

So do you know what I do?

I completely ignore my bathroom.

I clear the counters by throwing everything into a drawer or bin under the sink, then wipe it down and forget it. Until the next time I need a hair brush or tube of cream and have to face, once again, the disaster area that is my bathroom.

But this month is all about being brave and tackling our vices and learning to love what we have, which means that taking control of this bathroom space is crucial, so today our assignment is to conquer ours. Today we are going to organize our bathrooms!

The first time I did this challenge, I discovered that once I finally forced myself to get started, it really wasn't that bad. I started by emptying all the drawers and cupboards in order to figure out exactly what I had. I made piles of like items, and as I went, threw away garbage, expired items, and stuff I knew I'd never use.

Once everything was empty, I wiped down all the drawers and cabinets, then cut some pretty scrapbook paper to line the inside of my drawers, which were all stained and water-damaged. I couldn't believe what a difference such a small (and easy) change made! They're so cute now! I used scrapbook paper because that was what I had, but you could just as easily use pretty wrapping paper instead.

I then set about finding storage solutions for all my stuff. Items that I need but don't use that often—mani/pedi supplies, travel toiletries, sunscreen, and so on—went into gallon-size freezer bags, which I labeled clearly with a permanent marker then "filed" in a plastic storage bin I snagged from my pantry. You could just as easily use a box with the flaps cut off.

Bathrooms contain very oddly shaped items—like headbands and flat irons—which can be hard to store. Gooey gels, pastes, lotions, and hair accessories add to the general messiness of the situation. But don't worry—if I, a notorious bathroom organization avoider, can get a handle on it all, anyone can!

Even you!

First of all, clean your toilet and wipe down the bathroom. Then get together a trashcan, some cleaner, and any small contain-ers you think might help to organize drawers and under the sink. I found that vases, mason jars, and other containers work well, but you may prefer something else. The idea is to organize and see what you have on hand, so you can avoid buying yet an-other hairband (when you have 300 of them), tube of toothpaste (when you have three tubes in the back of the cupboard), or shampoo (even though you have seven mini-bottles that could get you through the whole month).

Here's my handy bathroom cleaning checklist, but feel free to customize it to your own needs and space.

bathroom
CLEANING *checklist*

BEFORE YOU START WIPE DOWN COUNTERS & CLEAN THE TOILET

BEFORE YOU BEGIN

Wipe down counters & clean the toilet--no one wants to hand out in a dirty bathroom!
- Make sure you have a large garbage can & recycle bin handy

EMPTY DRAWERS & CABINETS

Place like items together

TOSS THE FOLLOWING:
- Expired medication
- Any sunscreen or bug spray that is more than 2 years old
- Any half-used bottle that you know you will never use
- Anything that is broken
- Hotel samples you'll never use
- Dull tweezers, old applicators, etc.
- Ripped or worn out towels

SORTING & STORING:
Use gallon sized freezer bags to store items that you only need once in awhile:
Nail care items, travel items, or sunscreen
Label each one clearly with a permanent marker, then store in a box or bin

LINE YOUR DRAWERS WITH PRETTY PAPER

FIND CREATIVE STORAGE SOLUTIONS & WAYS TO STORE THE FOLLOWING:
- Makeup
- Hair accessories
- Bath toys
- Dental care
- Small tubes of ointment & cream
- Shower items

PUT IT ALL AWAY

PUT THINGS BACK:
- Put items neatly back in drawers/under counter
- Refold towels so they are uniform
- Keep counters as clear as possible--leave out only what you absolutely need
- Wipe counters & sweep floor

DEEP
cleaning
TASKS

Sort items every few months
Re-organize & label often
Toss unused/expired items often

Copyright Living Well Spending Less Inc www.LivingWellSpendingLess.com

Get Creatively Organized

Once you have your tools assembled, get to work! Empty the drawers and cabinets, and pile items together by category. Toss out anything that's expired (watch sunscreen, bug spray, and makeup). Get rid of anything that you don't plan on using again, as well as anything that's broken or worn out.

Divide the lesser-used items by category (nail care, travel, etc.) and sort into containers. Label containers and store in a box or bin in the cabinet. Line your drawers or cabinet shelves and store frequently used items in accessible locations. Consider creative storage solutions such as jars, vases, and other containers, and be sure to wipe off any lids or open items, so they stay clean in storage. Fold and put away towels and washcloths, ensuring each edge is going in the same direction.

I'm just like you—I throw it all in the drawer, wipe down the counter, and forget about it until I'm desperate for floss or a bobby pin. I have those little baskets, but getting everyone in the house to keep things where they belong is maddening. I will try labels next to see if that helps everyone stay on board with the clutter! —Meghan

Once everything's in place, give the bathroom another once-over, then sweep up the floor and you're done!

Doesn't that feel amazing? Great job!

Day 14: Reflection

Can you believe it? We've already made it through two weeks of zero spending! I'm so proud of you! I know the last few weeks have been full of challenges and hard work, but hopefully they've also been just a little bit fun as well.

> I finally organized my hobby closet so I can use it. It's been on my list forever—whew! My husband also went through his closet. It's been an amazing week. Thank you so much for the inspiration to stop spending and start using what we already have.
> —Steffanie

The first time we did this challenge, it was during a pretty stressful time in our personal life. I remember being so amazed at the out-pouring of love and support I received from our friends and family, particularly the ones who understood why we had decided to embark on a month of no spending.

I'm not sure if it was the fact that I was more aware and appreciative of their gestures, since I was trying to get by on less, or if there was a correlation to their giving and what was going on, but suddenly on Week 2 I started to feel very, very blessed. I noticed friends picking up the tab for me when we went for coffee, or offering to take my kids when I had an engagement, or stopping by with a bottle of wine and a little dinner.

Day 14: Reflection

It was amazing!

Perhaps when I'm in "normal spending mode" rather than "zero spending mode" I just overlook these little gestures or quickly reciprocate with money and forget about it. When I was committed to actions rather than spending, I started to be aware of and more deliberate in my gratitude and in the way I chose to give back. It truly did make me more appreciative of others.

Every day is a blessing, I believe, even though sometimes I may not feel it or see it. I have truly been taking in each challenge and letting them teach and guide me into better living habits, not only for myself, but also for my family, and my kids. What great life lessons they're learning by seeing me work hard at bettering myself and my home— our home. Thank you for this amazing journey you have created and shared with all of us! —Sylvia

---

Now is also a good time to reflect on what you've saved in the past two weeks. Compare your spending this month to last month and see if you can see a savings difference. I like to keep a little tally of how much I'm saving by comparing it to the previous month. It can be very motivating.

As you reflect this week on your zero-spending journey, what have you learned? What did you discover when you were cleaning out all those closets and drawers and examining the inner recesses of your home? Did you find any items you had completely forgotten you owned?

My house has gotten so much cleaner this week! It has been such an awakening as to how little it takes to keep my house clean if I just do a little at a time. The biggest blessing I experienced this week was when someone stopped by unexpectedly and I wasn't embarrassed about the state of my house, nor did I have to apologize for its state like I usually do. I'm hoping by the end of this month we will have a very firm grasp on our finances and how fast we will be able to get out of credit card debt! I'm so excited for what's to come! —Samantha

Take some time to write down these reflections and to give yourself a little credit for your effort!

Way to go!

WEEKLY *reflection*

What cleaning & organizing tasks did
you accomplish?

goals FOR NEXT WEEK

 What blessings have you
expierenced this week?

What has been the BIGGEST
struggle this week?

Where were you most tempted
(or where did you) CHEAT?

notes:

84

week
THREE

flex YOUR
CREATIVITY

Day 15: Refashion Your Clothes

Welcome to Week 3! I'm willing to bet that after all that cooking, cleaning, and organizing you are more than ready to have some fun! Well, me too!

And guess what? This week is going to be fun! (For free, of course.) The next few days are going to be all about flexing your creativity and repurposing all kinds of items using only what you have on hand.

So often when there's a problem, we try to buy the solution—when really, with just a little elbow grease or creative thinking, the answer is already near. Even if you aren't "crafty" per se, I have some pretty easy projects in store that will fit your taste and get your creative juices flowing.

And today, we are starting with our clothes!

Once your closets are organized, there are quite a few things you can make and do with your leftover items. Now I know most of your clothes are ready for consignment and Goodwill, but why not poke through the list at the end of this chapter and see if there are one or two treasures that you can create, just for fun?

I, for one, am not a huge sewer. Most of my sewing projects fall in the beginner-to-easy range, and I pretty much refuse to use a pattern. But you know what? I really enjoy sewing in small doses. When I started to search the web for ways to repurpose clothing, I couldn't wait to try some of these great ideas I found. I literally did a happy dance!

We're planning on doing a spending freeze starting tomorrow, so I'm reading up! I just learned how to sew, so I'm super interested in refashioning and making clothes. It's so much fun! —Lindsey

The idea behind refashioning clothes is pretty simple. With just a few alterations and modifications your old clothes can become new and exciting again!

If you're sick of a shirt, try cutting off the sleeves. If your husband is done with his button-down, try making it into a dress for your daughter, or if you have a surplus of t-shirts, try making one into a shopping tote. Not only are you giving old items new life, but you can even turn them into gifts and save bundles!

As I'm not terribly motivated to sew complicated projects, I was pretty excited to find so many resources online for refashioning clothes in simple and easy ways. I know you'll be as excited to try them as I was!

15 Awesome Refashioning Ideas

Get direct links to all 15 Refashioning Ideas at
www.LivingWellSpendingLess.com/LWSZresources

1. Turn Regular Jeans into Skinny Jeans (from Devon Alana Design)
2. Turn Polyester Granny Pants into Chic High Waist Pants (from Cotton and Curls)
3. Turn an Old Jumper into a Chic Belted Dress (from It's Always Autumn)
4. Turn a Shirt into a Ribbon-Tied Maternity Top (from DIY Maternity)
5. Turn Regular Pants into Chanel-Inspired Button Pants (from Freckles in April)
6. Turn Two T-Shirts into an Anthropologie-Inspired Top (from Life Is Beautiful)
7. Turn an Old Sweater into Cute Boot Socks (from Infarrantly Creative)
8. Turn an Old Sweater into a Cute Cardigan (from Instructables)
9. Turn Men's Slacks into a Pencil Skirt (from It's Always Autumn)
10. Turn a Men's Shirt into a Lace-Front Blouse (from It's Always Autumn)
11. Turn an Old Necktie into a Statement Necklace (from Green Eggs 'n Hamm/Wanderland Vintage)
12. Turn an Old Purse into Anthropologie-Inspired Bracelets (from At Second Street)
13. Turn Flip Flops and a Towel into Spa Slippers (from Crafty Nest)
14. Turn an Old T-Shirt into a Girls Ruffle Skirt (from Sew Much Ado)
15. Turn Regular Jeans into Maternity Jeans (from Crafty Cousins)

> I have never been much of a fashionista, but when my daughter gets home we will go over some of these ideas—she's a fabulous fashion queen!
> —Silvia

Which idea inspires you the most? Do you have any fun refashioning ideas of your own? Start by choosing just one project that really, truly inspires your creative side. You may be surprised to find how fun and easy refashioning can be!

15 AWESOME
REFASHIONING IDEAS

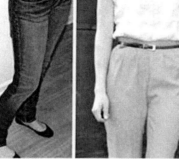

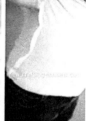

Day 16: **Get Fearlessly Crafty**

I have to admit—I'm a big fan of DIY. I love getting out the glue gun and paint and making something cute and creative. Nothing makes me happier than completely losing myself for an hour or two while I create something new. There is something about getting crafty that is just good for the soul.

But I'm going to let you in on a little secret: Not everything I make turns out wonderful. Not everything I make ends up on my blog or on Instagram or Pinterest. Most of the time I just don't show the world my failures!

One thing I've found in the blogosphere is that crafting can get more than just a little competitive. Oftentimes, people feel an immense amount of pressure to create something that turns out just like the picture. Listen, it's totally okay to create your own interpretation of any craft you see on a blog or online. Do your best and you'll be proud of the result!

Blogger Myquillen Smith's (aka "The Nester") motto for her home is "it doesn't have to be perfect to be beautiful," and I would like to point out that this truth also applies to DIY projects. It's okay to see a project you like on a craft blog or in a magazine and then modify it to work with the materials you happen to have on hand. Don't let the fear of it not looking exactly like the picture keep you from trying! Who knows? You might even like your version better!

The idea behind becoming fearlessly crafty is to create something out of the materials you have on hand. If we look back to our grandmothers' era when they'd decorate their homes using homemade quilts, braided rugs, or needlework, we see that most of the time, "DIY" evolved out of necessity and scarcity, not abundance. Their simple crafts added individual flair to a home and helped bridge the gap when purchased décor was something they'd have to forgo to make ends meet. With some simple yarn, fabric, or embroidery floss, they fashioned beautiful items to make a house a home. You can do the same!

> When I was little, my neighbor taught me to crochet by cutting up bread bags and crocheting them into carpets. It takes dozens of bags, but they last forever and are very spongy and comfortable to stand on. This is my favorite up-cycling craft!
> —Jacqueline

When I took my girls' toys away, we discovered an inner creativity and imagination that had been sadly forgotten. I saw my kids learn how to play and pretend again. Creating something during your zero-spend month will help you get into that same mindset.

You might not have all the exact supplies you need to create a certain craft—so be sure to improvise, don't buy! It's time to get creative. Again, even if you feel like it won't turn out perfectly, that's okay—give yourself permission to try, and see what becomes of it. The objective is to be fearless and have fun!

> Oh gosh, Ruth! This would require me to find my crafting supplies and glue gun—ha ha! We just haven't uncovered those boxes ... yet. But we almost finished the dining room makeover last night, so this has inspired me to try and come up with something crafty for the arch over the dining table. I'm just not sure what it will be yet! —Claire

I've assembled a few craft projects below, all of which require only items that I had on hand (so no spending)! Assess what you have and check out this list. I'm sure you'll find something that can get your creative juices a-flowin'!

20 Things You Can Make for Free

Get direct links to all 20 DIY projects at
www.LivingWellSpendingLess.com/LWSZresources

1. Ornament Wreath (from Eddie Ross Design)
2. Fabric-Covered Candle (from Living Well Spending Less)
3. Scrapbook Paper Tile Coasters (from The Love Nerds)
4. DIY Vintage Colored Glass (from Craftberry Bush)
5. Toilet Paper Roll Dahlia Art (from The Mayberry Home Journal)
6. I Heart [My State] Nail and String Art (from Our Mini Family)
7. Butterfly from Plastic Bottle (from Wonderful DIY)
8. Sewn Thank-You Cards (from Oh Hello Friend)
9. Children's Artwork Frames Gallery Wall (from Living Well Spending Less)
10. Book Page Wreath (from Creations by Kara)
11. Fabric-Covered Flower Pots (from Christine Chitnis)
12. Popcorn Kernel Wreath (from Cherished Bliss)
13. Towel Dish Mat (from Life in Grace)
14. Star-Shaped Crayons (from Living Well Spending Less)
15. Soup Can Vases (from Under the Sycamore)
16. Upcycled Ruffle Pillow (from Oh So Crafty)
17. Sharpie Mugs (from Living Well Spending Less)
18. Fall Book Page Garland (from Oh So Crafty)
19. Paint Chip Garland (from Cherished Bliss)
20. Simple Fabric Table Runner (from Living Well Spending Less)

Day 16: Get Fearlessly Crafty

> This is a great list of DIY projects! I am starting the 31 Day Challenge today. With some of these projects I would need to get materials, but that is fine—they can be for future frugal projects! Some are definitely doable without stepping foot in the store, and I love all of your ideas. —Michelle

Today your assignment is to make something using only what you already have, to get fearlessly crafty and create something new just for the joy of the process.

You can do it!

20 DIY PROJECTS
YOU CAN MAKE FOR FREE

$\mathcal{D}ay$ 17: Get a Free Education

What a fun week this has been so far! Hopefully with all of this DIY-ing and refashioning, your brain is starting to feel awake and alive and excited for each new challenge! It's time to start working on something enriching and even more stimulating ... it's time to learn something new!

Of course if you're familiar with student loans, books, and even the cost of private education, you're probably thinking, "Ha... education is far from free!"

Ah, but I'm here to tell you, you can always find ways to learn. Remember how we're getting creative this week? Well, sometimes education comes in different forms too. My husband Chuck and I went through Financial Peace University (part of the very inspiration for this challenge) a few years ago, and that was definitely an education, though in a different form. We study each week when we go to church. We learn about the world around us when we travel or read the news, or even from watching a documentary on Netflix. Lately I have loved getting new ideas and inspiration from free podcasts.

Life lessons aside, the education I'm talking about for today is mostly for your own enjoyment. Better yet—it's free! What have you always wanted to know more about? Below you'll find a list of 50 (yes 50!)

fun, free lessons that you can do right now, today, online. Escape into a little education, and you just may find yourself inspired, renewed, and revitalized—and more creative than ever before.

50 Free Online Lessons

Get direct links to all 50 online lessons at
www.LivingWellSpendingLess.com/LWSZresources

Hobbies, Crafts, and Games

1. **Learn how to sew an easy pillowcase dress**—make this cute dress in just a few hours using only a yard of fabric You can even donate your dresses to little girls in need (from Living Well Spending Less.)

2. **Learn how to knit**—watch these easy videos to master the technique. (from Knitting Help)

3. **Learn how to crochet**—links, videos, and info on basic stitches and easy patterns. (from Crochet.About)

4. **Learn how to take better pictures with your iPhone**—easy tips that everyone should know! (from Ashley Ann Photography)

5. **Learn how to take better portraits—10 amazing tips.** (from Digital Photography School)

6. **Learn some photography basics to improve your photographs—5 tips for taking better pictures with any camera.** (from Living Well Spending Less)

7. **Learn how to make homemade pickles**—step-by-step tutorial. Who knew it was so easy? (from Living Well Spending Less)

8. **Learn how to make a ruffle cake.** Watch this super-cool cake decorating video, then get the Martha Stewart recipe for Swiss Merengue Frosting to make it perfect!

9. **Learn how to play Bridge**—20 easy steps. (from WikiHow)

10. **Learn how to play Canasta**—I grew up playing this fun game with my family. Watch out, it's addicting! (from How Stuff Works)

11. **Learn how to play chess**—a combination of videos and written instructions. (from eHow)

12. **Learn how to tie-dye with natural ingredients**—use stuff you already have on hand! (Plus, get more natural dye ingredients and instructions from Money Crashers.)

13. **Learn how to make a freezer paper stencil**—this tutorial uses glitter, but you can also just use regular paint. (from Living Well Spending Less)

14. **Learn how to decorate with book pages**—The Nester shares 20 ideas for things you can make out of old books—cool!

15. **Learn how to draw**—cool video tutorials for how to draw all sorts of things! (from Drawing Now)

I did a Yahoo search: "How to Cross Stitch" (beginners). Do a search and find out how easy it is and how much fun. It's fairly inexpensive and rewarding. —Lisa

Self-Improvement

16. **Learn how to give a compliment**—if sometimes you just don't know the right thing to say. (from Life Optimizer)

17. **Learn how to remember names**—10 simple tricks. (from Forbes)

18. **Learn how to say you're sorry**—everyone could use a few tips on how to apologize. (from PsychCentral)

19. **Learn how to be a better listener.** (from Dumb Little Man)

20. **Learn how to make a great first impression**—because you never get a second chance. (from Positivity Blog)

21. **Learn basic etiquette for all situations**—8 basic tips everyone should know! (from Laurie Johnson)

Technology and Computers

22. **Learn how to edit photographs online**—a simple tutorial for getting started with the awesomeness that is PicMonkey. (from Blissful and Domestic)

23. **Learn how to start a blog**—This basic tutorial tell you everything you need to know about starting a blog for profit.

24. **Learn how to type faster**—the one-minute typing test is a little addicting. (from 10 Fast Fingers)

25. **Learn how to search online more effectively.** (from Alexandra Samuel)

26. **Learn how to use Pinterest to organize for the holidays (or any other event).** (from Creative Organizing Blog)

On Saturdays, almost every public library has at least one free program for kids. Not only that, they have free movies as new (to you, at least) entertainment ... there are all kinds of books and videos on how to do stuff, plus cookbooks! All while spending zero, as long as you get the materials back early or on time. —Barbara

---

Home Improvement

27. **Learn how to unclog a drain**—10 easy things to try. (from Wise Bread)

28. **Learn how to build a simple hanging bookshelf**—you could easily make this shelf out of scrap wood in the garage! (from Poppies at Play)

29. **Learn how to start a simple vegetable garden**—or start planning one for next season! (from Garden Guides)

30. **Learn how to prune a tree**—check out this simple video and never again wonder if you're doing it right! (from Land Designs Unlimited)

31. **Learn how to paint a room**—this step-by-step tutorial is great. (from ExpertRealEstateTips)

32. **Learn how to paint a piece of furniture**—I met Angela at a conference a few years ago and was so inspired to see all

of the cool stuff she was making from thrift store finds. I've yet to try it, but she makes it look super easy. (from Button Bird Designs)

33. **Learn how to sew on a button**—something everyone should know! (from Simple Sewing Projects)

34. **Learn to clean almost anything**—Heather Solos has a wealth of knowledge on all things domestic!

Traditional Education

35. **Take a free online course from the University of Washington**—choose from several different literature, history, and life skills courses. Very cool!

36. **Learn how to be a better writer**—start reading Jeff Goins' blog regularly and you'll practically get better through osmosis. Bonus: sign up for his e-newsletter and get access to his eBook too!

37. **Learn basic grammar skills**—Copyblogger shares 15 common grammar errors that make you look silly.

> MIT has open course work anyone can do/use. To get kids involved, look up home schooling resources (also a good way to help sharpen math skills). Don't forget there are tons of free Amazon Kindle books available for download on many different subjects too! — *Angie*

Life Skills

38. **Learn how to shop with coupons**—my "Beginner's Guide to Coupons" breaks it down to easy baby steps. (from Living Well Spending Less)

39. **Learn how to better manage your time**—10 tips for getting more out of each day. (from Living Well Spending Less)

40. **Learn how to speed clean your house**—keep things neat and tidy in just minutes each day. (from Living Well Spending Less)

41. **Learn how to perform CPR**—Watch the video ... it may help you save a life someday. (from CPRCertified)

42. **Learn how to perform the Heimlich maneuver ... um, ditto.** (from Howcast)

43. **Learn how to get started with investing**—3 great tips from Debt Free Adventure for how to start investing with $1000 or less.

44. **Learn how to drive a stick shift**—this video makes me think I might actually want to try! (from Jon Friedrich)

45. **Learn how to jump-start a car.** (from EricTheCarGuy)

46. **Learn how to make scrambled eggs**—something everyone should know! (from Living Well Spending Less)

47. **Learn how to be informed about what's going on in the world**—great tips if you ever felt overwhelmed by current events. (from WikiHow)

48. **Get prepared for the next election**—a nonpartisan website to help you make an informed decision.

49. **Learn how to negotiate**—simple tips for negotiating on almost anything. (from I Will Teach You to Be Rich)

50. **Learn how to make pretty iced sugar cookies**—impress your friends and have the perfect go-to gift, party favor, or treat for any occasion. (from Living Well Spending Less)

> To learn Spanish (or any other language for that matter) there's a website called Fluencia.com that offers free language classes. —Jen

Your assignment for today is simple: Learn one new thing.

It could be anything! Don't feel like you need to dive into all of these subjects at once. Simply pick your favorite and hit the books. Have fun!

Day 18: Find New Uses for Old Things

My goodness—can you believe we are already at Day 18? This week has been all about creatively using the things and resources we already have. So often we resort to running to the store for a solution or throwing out something before it's beyond its use.

Not only are these practices perpetuating the cycle of waste and causing environmental concerns, they're also perpetuating our own cycles of spending and consuming. Thinking outside the box and coming up with new uses for things we already have on hand helps us increase our appreciation and awareness for the labor and resources that go into the pieces of our day-to-day lives. It also helps us practice gratitude and break the cycle of mindlessly spending.

Many of us have taken on a zero-spending challenge out of necessity, not just as a way to engage in personal growth, but because, well, we're broke. We need to tighten our belts, pull up our bootstraps, and make ends meet. I realize that doing crafts, refashioning clothes, and watching YouTube videos aren't the answers to poverty or even overspending, but thinking creatively does help you become more mindful and deliberate in your actions.

Wouldn't it be nice to make a pretty tray, put some homemade cookies on it, and present that as a gift? —G

Take a moment to look around your home and ponder on the many things you have. If you're like me, your home is filled with comforts and items that reflect your family, their values and beliefs, and their likes and preferences. Consider something that you might not like anymore or that's no longer serving a purpose in its current state. This could be a clothing item, a kitchen item, or something else.

Is there a way that item could be repurposed into something else? Something that might beautify your home in some way, fill a family need, or simply give that item new life?

> I'm going to make patchwork cushions out of my clothes that are too pretty and groovy to throw away. It won't cost me a cent to add some new color to our existing spaces at home! Very excited to start this! —Nichole

Your goal today is to take a moment to beautify, upcycle, or repurpose something in your house.

Get creative and think of new uses for items you previously thought were at the end of their lives. Here are 21 ideas to get you started.

21 Clever Upcycling Ideas

Get direct links to all 21 upcycling ideas at
www.LivingWellSpendingLess.com/LWSZresources

1. Upcycled Crib into Magazine Rack (from Tip Junkie)
2. Toilet Paper Roll Wall Art (from How-To Gal)
3. Rake Wine Glass Rack (from Tattered Style)
4. Tin Can Lanterns (from Grow Creative)
5. Cookie Sheet Serving Tray (from Living Well Spending Less)

6. Cereal Box 3D Cardboard Star (from Grey Luster Girl)
7. Upcycled Sweater Pillow (from Infarrantly Creative)
8. Broke Crayon Monogram Art (from Upcycle Us)
9. Tuna Can Tealight Holders (from Practically Functional)
10. Upcycled Nightstand into Kid's Island Play Kitchen (from Paint on the Ceiling)
11. Paint Stirrer Garden Markers (from Living Well Spending Less)
12. Upcycled Books into Shelves (from Real Simple)
13. Pallet Plate Rack (from Apartment Therapy)
14. Upcycled Headboard into Chalkboard Welcome Sign (from Balancing Beauty and Bedlam)
15. Shutter Magazine Rack (from My Repurposed Life)
16. Woven Leather Belt Chair (from Saved by Love Creations)
17. Rain Gutter Kids Bookshelves (from Sunshine on the Inside)
18. Plastic Spoon Chrysanthemum Mirror (from Addicted 2 Decorating)
19. Mason Jar Herb Garden (from Camille's Style)
20. Wine Cork Bathmat (from The Crafty Nest)
21. Upcycled Spoon Ring (from Through the Front Door)

I love the cookie sheet idea, and the pillow, and the monogram letters made of crayons (so going to be the teacher end-of-year gift this year!). Can't wait to try some of these ideas! —Claire

---

Your assignment for the day: Look around your house with a keen eye and choose one item to either repurpose or breathe new life into.

Try to really examine all the things you have and see them in a new way. Are there any items you were considering purchasing at the end of your no-spend month that you could create on your own with what you already have? Which one of these projects inspires you the most? Pick one and run with it!

UPCYCLING
21 CLEVER NEW IDEAS FOR OLD THINGS

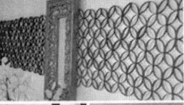

$\mathcal{D}ay$ 19: **Prepare to Pamper Yourself**

Here we are, very nearly done with Week 3! Hopefully you're feeling like you've learned a thing or two, you have a mild case of DIY fever, and you've been enjoying a productive few weeks of spending zero.

I know there have probably been more than a few difficult moments, but I hope you will be encouraged to know that we really are in the home stretch. Once again, I have to reiterate, you shouldn't feel like you have to keep up with every single challenge, every single day. The objective here is to give you some resources and ideas for alternatives to reaching for the credit card or running to the store. It's to help you get yourself into the savings mindset!

Today is going to be fun. This may surprise you, but I am a total spa girl! Back in the day, before I started blogging, I was the director of a large day spa in the Seattle area—yes, I actually managed a spa! Believe it or not, as part of my job description, I was required to receive regular spa treatments as part of employee evaluations and quality control. (In case you are wondering, yes, it was a pretty fun job!) I have to admit—there are times I really miss the days of frequent facials, massages, paraffin dips, and hair treatments!

We all deserve a spa day now and again—and it shouldn't be expensive.

Tomorrow, we have a special treat in store, but today, your goal is to create at least one of these homemade spa treatments. Many of these ingredients you probably have at home. If you don't have essential oils, you can always go with unscented versions. (If you're interested in purchasing essential oils, I highly recommend Young Living, but be sure to wait until your month of no spending is over! You can find out more about essential oils and how to use them here: http://www.livingwellspendingless.com/essential-oils-101)

> I love that these can be created from stuff around the house and that they're made to look so pretty!
> —Breanne

All of these treatments make great gifts as well, so make a double batch if you have the ingredients!

Who'd have thought you could treat yourself and someone else while spending zero?

Oatmeal Bath Sachets

These cute little oatmeal bath sachets can also be used in the shower. Oatmeal is great for soothing sensitive skin and helps add much-needed moisture during winter months.

Instructions:
1. Gather your ingredients—old-fashioned oats, a bar of soap, and the essential oil of your choice. I used lavender, but eucalyptus, lemon, peppermint, or bergamot would all be nice as well.

2. Use pinking shears to cut six small rectangles of thin fabric (approximately 4" x 6"). I used plain muslin, but you could use a pretty pattern or anything you have on hand. Placing two of the rectangles together, quickly sew around three sides to make a little cloth bag. Repeat for the other two bags. (Alternatively, you could use small organza party favor bags found in the wedding section at the craft or dollar store.)

3. Measure 1½ cups oatmeal into a bowl; use a knife to shave approximately 1 tablespoon of soap into oatmeal and then add 15–20 drops of your favorite essential oil. Mix well.

4. Carefully pour into prepared bags.

5. Sew shut the open side of each bag, then trim the excess to make a square shape.

Homemade Bubble Bath

I love taking bubble baths—the more bubbles the better—but I can't stand the artificial scents of most commercial bubble baths. This super-easy recipe uses a shampoo base. Try lavender for a relaxing bath. (It's great for bedtime baths for your kids too!) Or you can try eucalyptus for a soothing bath when you're sick.

Instructions:

1. Gather your ingredients—unscented (preferred) shampoo, ½ cup water, salt, and essential oils.

2. Measure ⅓ cup shampoo into a large measuring cup or bowl; add water and mix well.

3. Add 1 teaspoon salt and mix well until mixture thickens; add 15 drops of essential oil.

4. Pour into an 8 oz. jar or bottle; use 2 tablespoons per bath.

Honey Salt Scrub

This luxurious scrub is both exfoliating and moisturizing, a perfect combination for the dry winter months. I love it with peppermint or eucalyptus essential oils, but lemon or bergamot is also very refreshing.

Instructions:
1. Gather ingredients—olive oil, honey, salt, and essential oil of your choice.

2. Measure ⅓ cup honey into a measuring cup; add ½ cup olive oil; mix well.

3. Add approximately ¾ cup salt, a little at a time, mixing well until mixture reaches a thick but scoopable consistency. Add essential oil and mix well again.

4. Transfer to jar or other airtight container.

My first thought when I saw this was "Christmas gifts!" So cute—I love them all! I'm definitely going to have to pick up some essential oils—I seriously want to make the salt scrub, like, today! How adorable are the oatmeal bath sachets?! —Alisha

Honey Yogurt Oatmeal Mask

This exfoliating mask is great for most skin types. It uses only three ingredients, but must be kept refrigerated, as it contains fresh yogurt. It should keep in the fridge for approximately one week.

Instructions:

1. Gather ingredients—oatmeal, plain yogurt, and honey. (Note: for a less "lumpy" mask you can grind up oatmeal in a blender or food processor before using.)

2. Mix ⅓ cup honey with ⅓ cup yogurt. Blend well.

3. Add in approximately 1– 2½ cups oatmeal until mixture makes a thick paste.

4. Transfer to a jar or other airtight container. Will keep one week. To use, spread over face and let dry for 15 minutes. Rinse with warm water.

There you have it—four easy and luxurious recipes that use ingredients that you probably have on hand.

Your assignment is to create one homemade spa treatment today, then gather up any other relaxing bath supplies you already have and get ready for a spa day tomorrow! If you cleaned and organized your bathroom last week, you likely found some long-forgotten goodies like hotel lotions or fancy scented soap. Tomorrow you can put them to good use!

Finally, chill some water in the fridge (add some lemon, mint, or cucumber if you have any on hand), be sure your bathroom is clean, and get ready for some relaxation!

$\mathcal{D}ay$ 20: Have a Spa Day at Home

It's time to treat yourself! You've made it two-thirds of the way through the challenge. You've cleaned, you've cooked, you've created, and you've learned.

Today is the day we spa!

If you're thinking, "Um … Ruth? I only have a shower and I don't really like spa treatments" (I don't know who doesn't like spa treatments, but I'm sure you're out there)—well, that's just fine. What's your special treat? A good book? Sitting out in the sun? Listening to rock and roll and singing along in your living room? Whatever floats your boat, today is the day you do it! Have your fun—for free.

Your goal is to rest, relax, and recharge.

So often there's this mindset that saving money and spending less means you have to be poor and suffer. Yes, it's easy to spend money, and let's admit it—it's fun—but you don't have to punish yourself to feel like you're saving money.

A big part of living well and spending less—and discovering the good life—is being able to appreciate the things you have, and that means finding beauty in everyday moments. That also means taking care of yourself and allowing yourself to enjoy life. So go ahead, pamper yourself a little.

3 Ways to Pamper Yourself

Spa Bath

Supplies: oatmeal bath sachets, bubble bath, honey salt scrub, moisturizer, candles (optional).

Instructions: Light candles. Fill your bath with the warmest water you can tolerate; put in bubble bath and oatmeal sachet while tub is filling. Tie up your hair and apply your mask for a facial (see instructions below), if desired. Soak in tub for at least 15–20 minutes. Apply salt scrub all over then rinse with bath water. Dry off and then apply moisturizer while skin is still damp.

Spa Facial

Supplies: facial cleanser or soap, makeup remover, exfoliating facial scrub or washcloth, pot of boiling water, towel, honey yogurt oatmeal mask (or other mask of your choice), facial moisturizer.

Instructions: Wash your face and neck with the cleanser; remove makeup with makeup remover, if necessary. Gently exfoliate your skin with facial scrub or washcloth, using a circular motion around your face and neck. Rinse well. Turn heat off boiling water and hold your head above the steam for five minutes, using a towel over your head to trap the steam. Gently pat face dry, then apply a mask and let sit for 15–20 minutes. Rinse mask well, gently pat skin dry, and apply moisturizer, again in a circular motion all over face and neck.

Spa Manicure/Pedicure

Supplies: nail polish remover, cotton balls, emery board, nail clipper, cuticle trimmer (optional), nail brush or old toothbrush, homemade bubble bath, pumice stone, honey salt scrub, honey yogurt oatmeal mask, heavy duty hand/foot cream, nail polish, clear topcoat polish.

Instructions: Remove old polish from nails. Trim nails with clipper and then shape smooth with emery board. Trim cuticles, if necessary. Soak hands and feet in warm, soapy water for 10–15 minutes (or take a bath). Exfoliate hands and feet, applying scrub in a circular motion; use pumice stone to soften any rough or hard areas on feet. Pat dry, then apply mask and let dry for 10–15 minutes. Rinse well, then massage in heavy moisturizer. Wipe nails clean with polish remover, then carefully paint nails, letting polish dry for 5–10 minutes between coats. Finish with clear topcoat.

These are just suggestions. It's most important that you simply relax. This is your day to treat yourself and practice a little self-care. If you don't have all (or any) of the above supplies, just work with what you have and do something that makes you feel melty and relaxed.

Whatever you choose to do, enjoy. You deserve it!

The Honey Yogurt Oatmeal Mask was awesome! I did grind the oats first. The homemade bubble bath was great—I didn't have scented oil, but I had Root Awakening shampoo, so the "hint of tea tree" with some unscented Argon oil worked perfectly. —Claire

$\mathcal{D}ay$ 21: **Reflection**

It has been a very busy week. Productive, creative, fun, exciting, good ... but busy. My guess is that after three weeks of stretching yourselves, most of you are feeling downright exhausted and looking forward to a day of rest and self-reflection today.

For our Week 3 reflection, I want you to start thinking about both the past and the future. When you reflect on your struggles this week, consider what it was that brought you to the moment when you decided to commit to spending zero for this entire month. What do you plan to do in the future to save? Have you found any lifestyle changes that you think you're ready to make? How can you reuse things and be more mindful in the way you consume? What are your goals for next week?

> My goal is to make it to the finish line and get to the kids' room this coming week——and to finish the crazy garage! —*Claire*

I recently came across this quote that I found quite relevant and inspiring. It reminds us that we all have the power within us to shine. I had seen the first two lines before, but never the rest of it:

> Our deepest fear is not that we are inadequate.
> Our deepest fear is that we are powerful beyond
> measure. It is our light, not our darkness that most

frightens us. We ask ourselves, "Who am I to be brilliant, gorgeous, talented, fabulous?" Actually, who are you not to be? You are a child of God. Your playing small does not serve the world. There is nothing enlightened about shrinking so that other people won't feel insecure around you. We are all meant to shine, as children do. We were born to make manifest the glory of God that is within us. It's not just in some of us; it's in everyone. And as we let our own light shine, we unconsciously give other people permission to do the same.

—Marianne Williamson

So powerful!

Does this quote inspire you too? What did you love about this week? What was your biggest challenge?

WEEKLY *reflection*

 What creative projects did you tackle this week ?

 What were you inspired by this week?

goals
FOR NEXT WEEK

What has been the BIGGEST
struggle this week?

Where were you most tempted
(or where did you) CHEAT?

 notes:

Copyright · Living Well Spending Less Inc. www.livingwellspendingless.com

Keep your chin up—we're almost two-thirds of the way through
our month of Living Well and Spending Zero!

123

week
FOUR

earn money
& GET FREEBIES

$\mathcal{D}ay$ 22: Sell Your Stuff

I have good news! We've made it to the final full week of the 31 Days of Living Well and Spending Zero Challenge, and you are rocking it!

In Week 1, we focused on taking care of our basic needs (especially because hunger and boredom are the two main causes of mindless spending). In Week 2, we cleaned and organized our homes, learning to enjoy the space we're in, rather than trying to escape it. Then last week, we started to look at all the things we have in a new light, embracing our creativity and making new things out of old. This week our goal is to capitalize on our resources, both financial and emotional.

This week we're going to learn how to earn some extra money and discover new ways to get free stuff. It's going to be awesome!

After all, just because you're spending zero doesn't mean you shouldn't try to bank even more money and get free stuff while you're saving!

Today we're going to focus on selling stuff we don't need. Your first step is to go back to those "Sell" piles and bags of stuff you created in Week 2. (I've included a handy Stuff to Sell worksheet at the end of this chapter.) You probably had quite a few things you'd like to offload, but perhaps you weren't sure where to start or how to sell each type of item. Smart thinking! Different types of items are best sold in different marketplaces.

There are plenty of different options available for selling things, from eBay to Craigslist to Facebook—or you can even hold a good old-fashioned garage sale. Over the years, I've tried all four of these options with varying degrees of success. In fact, I recently made over $500 in just one month simply by selling stuff I no longer needed! You can too.

Here's what works, plus when and how to use these great options for selling your stuff

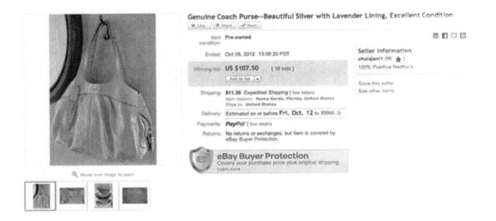

Sell on eBay

When to use eBay: eBay is your best bet for selling popular brand-name items (Coach, UGG, etc.) that are in very good or excellent condition, or high-value items that are specialized and hard to find. It can be great for collectable items (think vintage postcards or grandma's collection of brooches and pins), and unique memorabilia that has a specific target audience like sports memorabilia, breweriana, and souvenirs.

It's free to list items on eBay, but you will have to pay a commission if and when your item sells. Because you'll most likely need to ship your item, I also recommend planning ahead and considering the size and method of shipping before you list your item. You're responsible for anything that breaks or doesn't arrive in the condition promised, so bear that in mind before you box up those porcelain figurines without bubble wrap. Shipping is added to the cost of the item's bid, but customers can be put off by inflated shipping costs, so calculate carefully.

It's difficult to sell anything on eBay if you haven't established a reputation. However, it only requires a few experiences of buying, selling, and leaving feedback to boost your rating. If you have many items you're looking to get rid of that you think are "eBay friendly" (for example, if you just inherited Aunt Irma's thimble collection), it's definitely worth establishing a good rating.

> I have had wonderful luck selling toys on eBay; I have sold toys for more than I paid for them originally! I've sold everything from dishes to wallpaper border to a clock that I got $107 for. If I don't sell the item, it goes into the donation box. —Debbie

eBay Selling Tips

- **Take good pictures:** For the best shots, use indirect daylight (not bright sun) and no flash! Keep your background pleasant and simple, and be sure to take pictures from every angle. A white or light background works best. If the scale of an item is questionable, try using coins or another common item to establish size. When you photograph, always capture any flaws, dents, or scratches clearly. These often won't deter buyers as long as you're honest about them. (Read more about how to take better pictures in "8 Ways to Take Better Pictures," http://www.livingwellspending-less.com/2014/12/05/8-ways-take-better-pictures-2/.)

- **Choose the right category for your item and write a good description:** Be specific, otherwise potential buyers won't be able to find your listing! Do a quick search for similar items so you can categorize it properly, then categorize, name, and describe each item clearly. Be sure to mention the brand name in the title, along with the condition. Be as specific as possible; don't skimp on the details. Surprised buyers will give negative reviews if the item isn't found to be exactly as described. You should also mention if your item is coming from a pet-free or smoke-free home, and how it has been stored. If you carried a bag for one season or bought shoes for a wedding and only wore them once, mention these details in the description; it will help the buyer gauge the amount of wear and tear that they can expect. Research and use some of the lingo relevant to your item like NWT (new with tags) or NIB (new in box).

- **Consider selling "lots":** If you have clothing that's in good condition and it's all the same size, consider selling it in a lot. Title grouped items with the common thread and a description. For example: "girls size 6 play clothes in pastel colors." This can be a great way to sell items that are popular brands, but not quite designer (like GAP, American Apparel, or even Target). It's also a great way to sell children's clothing that's outgrown but still in good condition. Selling by lot can also be helpful for craft items (like fabric and scrapbook accessories) and small, similar items.

- **Make sure your item fits in the box before listing it:** I always keep on hand a few medium- and large-sized USPS flat-rate boxes, which are free from the post office. Always wrap your item well. (Again, you're responsible for anything that's damaged in shipping.) The rule of thumb with the post office is that it needs to be able to survive a ten-foot drop or twenty pounds of pressure.

- **Charge the USPS flat rate fee for shipping or calculate cost estimates first:** This way there are no questions about shipping and no surprises at the end. If you're shipping something that's breakable, add insurance to the shipping price or calculate the cost of shipping it through a UPS "Pack and Ship" service.

- **Answer buyer questions quickly:** Once your auction is live, be sure to pay attention to any questions that come up. (Be sure to check your junk folder too!) Answer all questions clearly and honestly right away. If it's a question about item specifics, post your answer publicly so other potential buyers can see the answers as well. This will also cut down on the time you have to spend answering buyers' questions via email.

- **Set a "Buy It Now" price:** In the early days of eBay, many sellers didn't set a minimum, so buyers were able to find treasures for cents on the dollar. The market has changed, and now many buyers prefer the option to "Buy It Now" rather than waiting and hedging their bets on a bid. Don't be afraid to set your minimum price at something that's low, but reasonable, and set the option for eager patrons to get their item on demand. Although many apps exist to help you manage your eBay account, eBay's Selling Manager is offered through the site and free to users. I recommend it for the average person.

> One tip I've seen is to search on eBay for the item you want to sell, look at the Sold listings for it or similar items, then calculate an average price based on the last five that sold. That gives you at least a ballpark sense of what the price should be.
> — Haley

- **Wait for payment before shipping:** Most buyers will pay quickly, but never ship an item until you've received your payment! You can easily send an invoice to remind buyers to pay. EBay payments are collected through PayPal, which is a secure site that helps ensure no one gets taken advantage of during the process. You can set up PayPal easily and link it to your checking or savings account so you can transfer the money as you go.

- **Ship your item as soon as possible:** As soon as you're paid, make an effort to ship your item as soon as possible. EBay makes this process very simple: you can actually pay for shipping and print your label at home. If you already have the box, then all you have to do is tape it up, slap on the prepaid label, and let your mail carrier pick it up, or drop it off at the nearest post office! EBay partners with UPS as well, if you prefer it to USPS.

- **Give feedback:** Be sure to write a positive note on your buyer's feedback page. EBay is driven by ratings, and your score is very important to boosting your profile and encouraging buyers to use you in the future. For larger retailers and eBay professionals, the occasional bad review or unhappy customer won't make or break them. However, reviews can be key for the private seller who is just unloading a few items from home. If you leave positive feedback for your buyer, they will hopefully then return the favor so you can have even more successful sales in the future! If days pass and you haven't heard from them, it doesn't hurt to send a follow-up message and request feedback.

Sell on Craigslist

http://craigslist.org

When to use Craigslist: Whereas eBay is a carefully regulated and secure way to sell your items, Craigslist is much less restricted. It targets a local audience, so it's a great option for selling items that you wouldn't want to bother with shipping, including furniture, toys, and other household items. You can find buyers for leftover tile, yard and landscape items, appliances, and more.

Maclaren Twin Triumph Double Stroller-Green - $100 (Punta Gorda (PGI))

Date: 2012-09-29, 5:48PM EDT
Reply to: your anonymous craigslist address will appear here

This double stroller has served us well but our girls are now too old to be carted around. **sniff** This particular model sells for $295 new and is in excellent condition, no rips, stains, or broken parts of any kind. It includes a rain guard, which in my opinion is the best part, as it has saved us (& our stuff) from getting drenched during a sudden summer thunderstorm more than once. I am very tall (over 6') so I chose this model because it has the highest handles of any double stroller on the market. However, it is also very comfortable for shorter pushers too. :)

From the Amazon.com description:

These all purpose go fast buggies for two have a high-performance aluminum frame and feature a one-hand compact umbrella fold, a height adjustable 5 point harness for added security and has multiple reclining positions with adjusting straps. The double swivel wheels are lockable in the front and have an easy to use central foot brake. Other features include ergonomically optimized, three-position, height adjustable handles; a removable, washable seat, handy mesh shopping basket and a carry strap for easy portability. The Twin Triumph includes a rain cover and two independent, water resistant hoods with UV protective viewing windows to allow little ones the chance to view the world regardless of weather pattern. Measures 33.5" L x 24.5" W x 41.8" H. Weighs 23.4 pounds.

You won't get the best price on items with a targeted audience, like collectables (unless they're very locale-specific like high school sports memorabilia), but you'll get a wider audience than you would with a Facebook or yard sale. Think of Craigslist as the "Buy/Sell/Trade" classifieds section of newspapers back in the day. The big appeal to local buyers? Large items like furniture are easy to pick up.

Due to the unregulated nature of Craigslist, I'd shy away from selling small valuables, like jewelry or designer handbags. Buyer interaction is often face-to-face, and after a friend relayed to me a particularly harrowing story about picking up a cat tree in a scary situation, I'd advise that you proceed with caution. I always make sure that my husband is home when a buyer picks up an item, and I don't give out my home address on the first email interaction.

Craigslist is free, which makes it an easy way to list your items. It's definitely more popular in some areas than others—I had way more success selling on Craigslist in the Seattle area than I do in Southwest Florida. Metropolitan areas, cities, and college towns seem to see the most success with Craigslist. It's very easy to put up a listing though, and there's no reason not to give it a try!

> I find people coming to garage sales are looking for really, really cheap prices. It might also depend on the neighborhood, but I can sell my stuff on Craigslist for a better price. I also got good deals on Craigslist for some household items without having to travel around town for garage sales. I used to sell on eBay before I got on Craigslist. There is the "going to the post office" side of it. For me, it's much more practical to have people come and pick up stuff. —*Practical Mama*

Craigslist Selling Tips

- **Write a good description:** Be sure to mention the brand name in the title, along with the condition and age. Be as specific about the details as possible. You'll want to include the amount of wear and tear on the item, particularly furniture, and mention if it's from a smoke-free and pet-free house. In your description, consider mentioning the style such as "mid-century modern" or "art deco," as well as the materials (laminate, solid oak, etc.). Occasionally buyers will search nearby areas and be willing to travel for the right item that meets their style. Isn't it more appealing to purchase a "quality contemporary end table with beautiful white laminate finish" than "white end table"? In addition, you should include a message in your listing that all sales are final.

- **Take good pictures:** (see above)

- **Don't set your price too high:** We'd all like to think our stuff is worth close to what we paid for it, but the sad truth is that used stuff isn't worth all that much. Do a search for your item to find out what other people are asking. If your price is significantly higher, don't expect any calls. Take into consideration the value of someone picking up the item and moving it themselves, a service which can almost be more valuable than the item. When selling appliances, electronics, and furniture that would otherwise be costly or difficult to dispose or get rid of, offering a lesser price may be worth it. Leave room for bargaining (a common practice on Craigslist), but hold out for the price you want. Be sure to decide on your agreed-upon price before meeting face-to-face.

- **Don't overlist your item:** Follow the Craigslist rules or your post will be flagged and all your listings will be removed. Each region is slightly different, but as a general rule you can post any given item once every seven days.

- **Stay safe:** Unfortunately there are some weirdos out there. To be safe, communicate through Craigslist rather than using your personal email. If your item is small, meet in a neutral public location, and if you're having a buyer come to your house, arrange for someone to be home with you.

I had a lot of items to sell, so I started selling them on Craigslist, but I also started a free website at blogspot.com. For every item I listed on Craigslist, I referenced the website so they could click on it and see all of the items I had for sale. I have such a range of items for sale that hopefully while someone is looking for boys' shoes, they notice a light fixture they need! —*Jenny*

Sell on Facebook http://www.facebook.com

When to use Facebook: Facebook is free and super easy, so there's really no reason not to try Facebook first. These days almost every city has a local selling group. Once you join, snap a picture and list a price. (Follow the same selling tips as the Craigslist tips listed above.) If you can't find a group to join, you may want to ask around to see if any of your local friends have heard of one, or you can simply post your item on your own Facebook wall. If it doesn't sell you can always try Craigslist or eBay.

The obvious drawback is that you're only appealing to your Facebook friends list or to the members of the selling group. Still, as a free service and a safe, easy method, Facebook couldn't be simpler. Ask friends to share your listing, especially if you're in a hurry to sell (if you're moving, for example). Viral marketing is powerful, and social media can be a great tool to get the word out and find your market.

> Facebook yard sale pages are wonderful in my area. Not only do I usually sell my stuff pretty quickly, but I have made some wonderful friends. If you set up a FB yard sale page for your town, county, or community, be sure to have clear rules and enforce them. At the same time, keep it friendly so people will enjoy visiting. —Mara

Hold a Garage Sale

When to throw a garage sale: If you have a lot of stuff to sell and you live in a great neighborhood for garage sales (close to a main street, lots of drive-by traffic, etc.), then a garage sale might be a good option.

If you're looking to make money quickly, bear in mind, garage sales can take a lot of planning and effort. Craigslist, eBay, and Facebook can be quicker, easier, and faster in terms of simply unloading a few items. However, if you're ready for a cleanout, a garage sale might be the way to go.

I hosted a "freebie" party once for our school group just before Christmas. Each family brought as many items as they wanted to the party, and the children then got to choose Christmas gifts for their loved ones from the stash! It was so much fun and easy to host. A friend is hosting a similar event next month—her "freecycle" party! —Mrs. J

Garage Sale Selling Tips:

- **Set prices to move and make them clear:** Get some tags and mark items to move. Be prepared to make some deals and throw in some extra items to sweeten the deal. Garage sales are often hit heavily in the morning (when the selection is the best) and then start to dwindle down as the day wears on. You can attract shoppers throughout the day by advertising 50 percent off at a set time of day, or try offering 2-for-1 deals to keep things moving. Make sure your prices are clearly marked in large writing.

- **Pick a prime date:** Does your neighborhood do a rummage tour? Is the local fair in town and driving traffic through your area? These are great times for you to plan your sale. Base your marketing on the times when your area of town is the most popular. If you live in a college town, consider a sale the weekend that campus opens to attract students seeking furnishings and décor.

- **Use advertising and signage:** Put those artistic and creative skills to use by making some big ol' signs and posting flyers, and if it's a nice day, put most of your goods outside the garage. Many garage sale patrons are impulse stoppers, so be sure that that they can see you're offering a great reason to get out of the car.

- **On the day of the sale, start early:** Prime rummage sale hours start at 5 a.m. Yes, you read that right. Early-morning bargain hunters get up at the crack of dawn to get the best deals. So make sure you reach dedicated garage sale shoppers by starting your sale bright and early.

- **Enlist help:** Enlist the help of your neighbors, friends, social media network, husband, and kids. Let your kids try their hand at making signs, posting prices, or selling and making change to teach them how buying and selling works. Get friends to spread the word. If a friend or neighbor has a few items to sell, let them join you, with the caveat that they take it back with them if it doesn't go. (You don't want to make your yard the dumping ground for everyone's stuff!)

- **Donate and eliminate leftovers:** When you've finished your yard sale, count out your earnings and round up your remaining items. Inventory what you have left and determine whether it realistically belongs in the trash or if you can donate it to Goodwill, a women's shelter, a preschool, or another charity in your area.

Now go sell something!

STUFF to sell

USE THIS WORKSHEET TO BRAINSTORM STUFF YOU CAN SELL

ITEMS TO SELL	PLACES TO SELL	ASKING	SOLD

Copyright © Living Well Spending Less, Inc. www.LivingWellSpendingLess.com

$\mathcal{D}ay$ 23: Get Free Money

Have you ever gotten to the end of the month and thought to yourself, "Where the heck did all my money go?" (If not, then you are clearly a much better money manager than I am!) Life can get hectic and it is easy to lose track of our money sometimes, but chances are you've got at least a little money hidden out there somewhere, or you are missing an opportunity to make some. Today we're going to find it!

Did you know that on average, people have $90 in loose change just lying around their house? It's true! And there's even more free money to find out there—you just need to know where to look.

4 Ways to Get Free Money

Go on a Money Hunt

Today is the day to check all those pockets ... and more. Go through your change jars, couch cushions, the console and glove compartment in your car, and any other sneaky places where money hides, and count it up! You aren't spending, but you can be finding!

My kids simply love doing this—we all go on a money hunt and sort through any places we can think of where money hides.

What about those old coat pockets? How about purses? Or the laundry pile?

Once you've gathered all the change you can find, take it in to your local bank. Though nowadays most banks accept loose change, if yours doesn't, you'll have to put it into rolls or trade it in at a Coinstar machine. (You can find the nearest Coinstar right from the homepage of their website: https://www.coinstar.com/.) Just keep in mind that they'll charge a commission, unless you trade in your coins for a grocery card (which can be handy!) or store credit.

Find Forgotten Gift Cards & Credit

Gift cards and certificates are pretty easy to lose track of. So it's time to search the bottom of your purse, your junk drawer, and wherever you keep old birthday cards. Whether they are Scrip cards you bought from your school fundraiser or other items you've received or purchased and forgotten, the first thing you want to do when you find them is determine whether they have a balance. To check, simply call the number on the back. Then write the dollar amount right on the front with a Sharpie.

Don't forget about e-gift cards as well! If you're a member of Swagbucks (http://www.swagbucks.com) or Restaurant.com (http://restaurant.com), or if you subscribe to group coupon sites like Groupon (https://www.groupon.com) or LivingSocial (https://www.livingsocial.com), you might have a few items you purchased and then forgot about or have yet to redeem. (Guilty as charged, right here!)

Go through your inbox and search words like "credit," "certificate," and "redeem" to see if you have anything floating around. I like to keep a folder on my desktop to track these items, but now's the time to get a filing system in place so you can remember them for future use.

Some insurance companies, like Humana, offer member benefits that allow you to redeem activity points for gift certificates. Many credit card companies also offer points and benefits for members. You may just have a few assets that you didn't even realize!

> Thank you so much for this post. It reminded me that I had bought a couple of Restaurant.com gift certificates a few months ago that I had completely forgotten about! I am putting my kids on a loose change hunt as soon as they get home from school. —Susan

Earn Swagbucks

As I mentioned above, Swagbucks is an online service that gives you credit for searching the web or for printing coupons (http://www.livingwellspendingless.com/saving-money/swagbucks/). You simply search the web using the Swagbucks search engine to earn credits ("swagbucks") that you can trade in for gift cards to online retailers like Amazon or brick-and-mortar retailers like Starbucks. You can also earn credits by taking quizzes, watching videos, and printing coupons.

While you won't earn a fortune at Swagbucks, it doesn't hurt to get a little free money for something like surfing the web, which we all know you were going to do anyway ... right?

Check Out Other Free Money Sites

There are a number of other sites like Jingit (http://business.jingit.com), Recyclebank (https://www.recyclebank.com), InboxDollars (http://www.inboxdollars.com), and Ebates (http://

www.ebates.com) that allow you to earn money while you shop, surf the web, take short surveys, watch videos, or give consumer opinions. Those I've mentioned seem to have better results than some others that can send you on endless "spam odysseys" all over the Internet.

Obviously, spending money to earn or save money is not recommended (seeing as you've committed to spending zero), but it doesn't hurt to sign up and see if you can generate some income without shopping!

Don't forget about returning (new) things that you bought, but didn't need, to the store. Usually you can only get a cash refund if you still have the receipt, but you may be able to get store credit if you return it without a receipt and provide your ID. —Tina

---

Today's assignment is to get creative and think up all those hidden bonuses. Make a comprehensive list to track all that free money you might miss out on or lose track of!

$\mathcal{D}ay$ 24: Get Free Stuff

I've said it before and I'll say it again: What's better than free? There is just something so thrilling about getting something for nothing, whether it be getting a free sample, finding a treasure, or discovering something that costs you nothing—like the universe just handed you a little present! Yesterday we talked about some great places to find free money; today we are going to score free stuff.

Just as a side note—just because something is free, that doesn't mean you always need to take it. That's an easy way to end up with a bunch of crud you really don't need. One man's trash can be another man's treasure, but it can also still be trash. So resist the urge to clutter up your house with a lot of "free" treasures that require your attention (furniture that needs a lot of repair, items you intend to repurpose, but never quite get to, and so on). Also stay away from free samples of things you just don't like. Though free is tempting, taking what you don't like is silly. Give yourself permission to say no occasionally.

I love free stuff! I like that you posted a warning about not getting something just because it's free—I am so guilty of that, especially with coupons! —Amanda

Still, there are plenty of great free things out there to be found! If you put out requests to friends, your church, and your family, you may be amazed at all the resources you can find.

5 Great Sources for Free Stuff

Amazon.com

Amazon has so many great deals and great ways to shop. One thing you may not realize is that every day Amazon gives away a huge selection of Kindle books, MP3 music, and Android apps. If you don't have a Kindle, that's okay—you can download the Kindle app for your smartphone or device and read away!

I check the following pages frequently for freebies:

- Top 100 Free Kindle Books
- Artists on the Rise FREE MP3 Music Deals
- Amazon App Store

For Free Kindle books, I love http://ereaderiq.com. You can import your wish list from Amazon.com and track books you want. I got all my eBooks free (or some for 99 cents when the price drops). —Paula

Free Product Samples

I'm not just talking about going to Costco on sample day! Sites like Freebies 4 Mom (http://freebies4mom.com) are dedicated to offering hassle-free, legitimate samples and deals you can sign up for. If there are particular products you're interested in or something new you'd like to try, you can also try to contact the company directly. So few consumers do this—yet many companies are often willing to give a free sample to an interested buyer.

Extreme Couponing Freebies

If you've watched anything on couponing (like TLC's Extreme Couponing) you've probably wondered how on earth they end up getting so many things for free. While those shows are scripted and planned out months in advance, there are plenty of day-to-day ways to get free items when you pair high-value coupons with store sales.

For more on how to coupon, check out my Beginner's Guide to Couponing to get started (www.LivingWellSpendingless.com/bgtcoupons). It can seem a little challenging at first, but you've got a little planning time before you step in a store again, so now is a great time to check it out!

Freecycle & Craigslist

Freecycle.org (https://www.freecycle.org/) and Craigslist.org (http://www.craigslist.org/about/sites) are two online "classified ad" services that often have hundreds of items listed for free! Also be sure to check Facebook for neighborhood groups or local "Mommy Swap" groups you can join. Check the community boards at your local university, at your child's school, or at other local institutions as well. You can practically find anything for free—you just need to look!

Your Local Library

Just in case you've forgotten, right down the street from most of us, there's a place where you can access thousands of books, magazines, movies, and music for free! Local libraries have come a long way in terms of their offerings, and many have free classes, free meeting rooms or conference areas, and free activities for kids as well as adults. Simply by signing up for a library card and remembering to return your books on time, you can literally have the world at your fingertips. Many libraries now offer Zinio (http://www.zinio.com) for magazines, which are easily downloaded to your tablet or e-reader.

Last Saturday my neighborhood was having over fifty yard sales. I waited until the sales were packing up for the day and we drove up and down each alley until we found some fun freebie furniture that had been discarded! I found a new dresser and a new desk! —Kim

---

What are your favorite freebies?

$\mathcal{D}ay$ 25: Try Bartering

Twenty-five days into this crazy (as in, crazy awesome!) spending freeze, you might be starting to miss one or two things. Or ten. Or fifty. Just a little bit. Or a lot. Perhaps even desperately.

And that's okay. It's normal. If you don't miss anything you either (a) are cheating, (b) had way too much stuff to begin with and should probably keep your spending freeze going until you start to feel the pain, or (c) are one of those people who could happily subsist on nothing, in which case you probably didn't need to go on a spending freeze in the first place. (Just saying ...)

> I know for us, the spending freeze opened our eyes to some unconscious areas of spending that we didn't even realize—like picking up a soda whenever we went to the gas station, or buying a magazine at the checkout line. —Betty

It's those little things you buy that can add up almost as much as a weekly movie habit or restaurant visit. So what have you learned so far? What's been your biggest challenge?

Of course, if you are anything like me, you may be, for the most part, enjoying this challenge of seeing just how much you can do without. It is forcing you to view your approach to money and stuff in a slightly different way, and while it might not always be sunshine and roses, you can see the benefit, feel the benefit, and the sacrifice is worth it.

Until, of course, there is something you really, really, really, really want (but don't necessarily need), like a night away from the kids or a Starbucks latte or a bite of chocolate or Just. One. Beer.

Yesterday we talked about how to get something for nothing. Today we are going to get something for something. Today you're going to learn how to trade things you have for what you want! If that sounds scary, take heart. You do not have to be a swap meet pro to barter! It can be as painless as a simple trade with a friend. The key is to figure out what you have to offer that someone else would want. It can be as easy as exchanging babysitting with a friend or doing the dinner swap that we talked about back on Day 4.

Believe me, everyone has something! Is there a particular thing you're good at, or something you cook or bake that everyone loves? Do you love to clean, or could you babysit for the afternoon? Do you have a talent or skill you could share, such as photography or sewing or knitting? Do you have extra food or toothpaste or razor blades in your stockpile, or too many jars of homemade jam in your pantry? Do you have any gently used books or electronics or clothing you're ready to pass to a good home? Are you willing to run errands or paint or be a handyman for an afternoon? Think hard. You've got something.

I love the bartering system. I'm a personal trainer and I have been able to trade my services for housecleaning, massages, and legal services (having a living trust done). Such a great deal! — Kathy

---

Think about what you're good at and get ready, because we're about to make a deal! Once you come up with your plan, the first place to tap into is your own network. This might mean asking a neighbor or a fellow parent, or putting up an ad on your church bulletin. To get you going, here are six other ways you can find a barter partner.

Facebook

Easy, free, and (very) frequently checked, Facebook is a great place to post your bartering offers. I posted this on one particularly desperate day:

Ruth Hollander Soukup
October 13 near Punta Gorda

Spending Freeze, Day 48: It has come to this....I am desperate for two things & ready to barter. Here are the things I have to offer:

-a family photo session to take your Christmas card photo
-a home baked chocolate cake with ruffled meringue buttercream frosting
-a beautiful custom handmade "pillowcase"-style fall dress for your little girl

Here are the things I am asking for in return:
-beer
-babysitting

Any takers? :-)

Like · Comment

🖒 Stacy Zientarski, Serrin Boys and Patricia Crowley Lopes like this.

💬 View all 21 comments

Despite a little teasing from some friends, let me tell you—I had many offers for both babysitting and beer, and a very happy husband!

It's okay to be cheeky with your post, especially if it's something small. If you're nervous, have a little fun with it. Friends will respond happily and helpfully, I promise. If bartering isn't in your "comfort zone," all the better—if bartering is unusual for you, your friends will be much more likely to respond quickly and kindly.

If you decide to aim for something a little higher than just beer and babysitting (professional services like editing, computer programming, or consulting; or an extended stint of dog-sitting, help with moving, or labor-intensive yard work), be prepared to pony up with equal or better services. Typically the "asker" needs to bring something lucrative enough to the table to entice the "giver" to give.

Remember, you're trying to get someone to forgo pay, so you need to make it worth their while. Gone are the days when you could entice college buddies to move your stuff with a promise of pizza and beer. As adults, we probably have to be a little more generous and reciprocate manual labor—so be prepared to roll up your sleeves and get to work. Bear in mind that you're still getting what you need without spending a dime.

Garage Sales

Customarily, garage sales happen because people want to get rid of things (not accumulate more). A while ago, I read this great post from One Hundred Dollars a Month (http://www.onehundreddollarsamonth.com/how-to-barter-for-food-like-pilgrims-and-indians/), where blogger Mavis and my friend Amber (from Coupon Connections (http://couponconnections.com) went around to garage sales dressed as a pilgrim and a native American to barter and trade. All in all, they were quite successful in snaring kitchen items, garden items, and more in return for groceries and items from their garage sales.

Dressing up in costumes and running around your neighborhood might not be for everyone, but try having a little fun the next time you go to a garage sale. Instead of offering cash, think of what you have, and put it on the table—"I would really like this umbrella stroller for my two-year-old daughter. I see that your son has outgrown it, and my eight-year-old son has a perfect set of rollerblades that no longer fit him. Could we trade the blades for the stroller? I'll bet your son would be the right age." See how easy it is?

Craigslist

Back to the resource that is Craigslist. While Craigslist has gotten some bad press over the past few years, it can also be an amazing resource (as long as you use some common sense when dealing with strangers!) Often our barter section is filled with larger items (trade a small boat for a surfboard), but it's certainly worth posting smaller items on there to see if anyone bites. The great thing about Craigslist is that people are in the buy/sell/trade mindset already so they're looking for commerce opportunities.

U-Exchange and Time Banks

U-Exchange (http://www.u-exchange.com) is a similar "listing" service that's free to use and 100 percent based on bartering. In one column, you can view all the listings in your area and the services that person is offering. In the other column, you can view what they're seeking. Neat! You can find almost anything listed from children's toys to dental care to marketing and consulting services.

Another site to check out if you're really into bartering is Time-Banks (http://www.timebanks.org). The way that time banking works is: say Person 1 needs landscaping services and is willing to trade photography services. Person 2 wants photography, but is a yoga teacher. Person 3 would trade some catering services for yoga lessons, and Person 4 is a landscaper in desperate need of a caterer. (Whew.) So, each person "banks" their time and uses it on a pay-it-forward principle. Typically time banks vary by region and are run and managed by community organizations. They often require members to "bank" a certain amount of time each month, quarter, or annually to keep the bank operating.

Neighborhood Exchanges

Perhaps your neighborhood has a babysitting co-op, food exchange, or other service. Many communities are listed on the Food Swap Network (http://foodswapnetwork.com), Babysitting Co-op (https://www.babysittingcoop.com), or are listed in groups on Facebook. Even if your neighborhood isn't listed, you can find guidelines on how to host your own community swap or co-op. If you put up pickles this year and would like to exchange them for tomato sauce, this might be your best bet!

Host a Swap Meet Party

I love hosting a good party! While you're on your spending freeze, parties can seem like a thing of the past, but you know what? You can host a frugal, thrifty, and fun swap meet party! First pick a theme—an accessory or clothing swap would be great to give new life to the things you cleaned out on Day 12, or try a kids' toys or clothes exchange for your items from Day 10. Perhaps you have a friend that has fabric but no ribbon or a friend who has a bunch of chalkboard paint—and let's say you have a gazillion tiles for coasters. Have a "craft swap" and tell everyone to bring a component or two and host an afternoon of crafting.

To do it for free, make it a potluck and clean out the recesses of your liquor cabinet to make a fun signature drink. (Consult a mixologist app to see what can be made with say, bitters, Amaretto, and brandy, or just make it BYOB.) Light a few candles, put on some music, and voila—you've got a party with zero dollars spent.

I'll warn you ... bartering gets a bit addicting! You may have so much fun doing a clothing swap, or your husband may be so thrilled with your Craigslist finds that you'll become a bartering expert! See what you can trade for, today!

$\mathcal{D}ay$ 26: Enjoy a Free Date Night

So this week we've found ways to get free items, earn a little extra money, and we started to barter, so now it's time to shift our focus and look at how we can spend a little time with our loved ones for free.

As I discussed in Day 20 when we had a spa day, just because you're saving money doesn't mean you need to feel like you're "punishing" yourself. You still deserve to have enjoyment, happiness, and caring in your life. All of us do. Part of that includes our relationship with our spouse or significant other. Even if you're a single parent, you still need a night out once in a while!

Unfortunately, nights out can cost money. Dinner and a movie (with a babysitter, a glass of wine at dinner, and popcorn during the flick) can set you back almost $100. Yikes! It's time to get creative! Spending time with loved ones is good for your health, and theirs. It gives you an opportunity to reconnect, and it's critical for the vitality of your marriage or relationship (or even friendship).

Yesterday you mastered the art of bartering, so you should have babysitting taken care of. If for some reason you don't—that's your first goal. Secure babysitting so you can get away and enjoy a little time one-on-one! Then use one of these ideas to create a memorable date.

29 Creative Free Date Ideas

1. **Go stargazing—find a place away from the city lights.** Bring a blanket and pillows so you can cuddle while you soak in the night sky. Make the evening even sweeter with a thermos of homemade spiked cocoa!

2. **Tour a local winery or brewery**—some breweries and many wineries offer free tours, which usually include a sample or tasting at the end!

3. **Donate blood together and get a free movie ticket**—I'm not sure if this is done anywhere else, but in my town any time you donate blood you receive a free movie ticket. Why not make an evening of it? First do some good and then enjoy a free movie (plus you get free cookies at the blood bank)!

4. **Volunteer together**—serve at a local soup kitchen or food bank, spend a day building together for Habitat for Humanity, or simply spend a few hours picking up litter in a neglected area of town. There are so many opportunities for giving back!

5. **Go hiking**—this is one thing I really miss about the Pacific Northwest! Research local trails, then head off to explore. For most trails you won't need any special gear, just comfortable shoes and a backpack with water and snacks.

6. **Do a crossword together**—before kids, this used to be our favorite Saturday morning activity! We'd cook a big breakfast then break out the crossword puzzle, refusing to give up until we'd filled in every last square.

7. **Have a picnic in the park**—pack a few treats and a bottle of wine and spend the evening dining alfresco at your favorite park. Even when the weather gets a little cooler, this is a great option. Just take a few extra blankets for cuddling!

8. **Cook or bake together**—why not spend the evening trying out a brand new recipe? You could learn to bake bread from scratch, make cookies, or simply prepare and share a meal. If you want to "eat out" at home you could attempt a few of the restaurant copycat recipes from Day 5.

9. **Attend a free concert, speech, or book reading**—most communities have free events happening every week, whether it's a free concert in the park, a reading at a local bookstore, or a speaker at your library or university. Check out your library, chamber of commerce, and colleges online, or a local paper to see what's going on.

> I went to a free piano concert at noon today, and they had a special guest "international virtuoso"! The two-piano group hosts a free lunchtime concert on the last Friday of the month. Yes, it's a weekday and at noon, but if you can get away there's a free date, or a lunch with the girls! —Dolores

10. **Attend a free art show**—explore the works of up-and-coming artists by touring one **or two art galleries in town.** In addition, many art museums offer free entrance nights for community members.

11. **Play a game**—board games and card games are such a nice way to spend time as a couple. Even puzzles can be fun! Our favorite two-person games include Scrabble,

Bananagrams, Skip-Bo, Phase 10, and Canasta (played with two decks of playing cards).

12. **Have a movie night at home**—watch a favorite movie you already have, or check one out for free from the library. Most libraries have an extensive selection of movies to choose from. Make it special by adding homemade popcorn, hot chocolate, fondue, or other goodies.

13. **Visit a farmers market or street fair**—spend a morning checking out the work of local artisans. Many food booths give out free samples of their wares, and there's often music or entertainment going on as well.

14. **Go for a drive**—if you live in a relatively scenic area, spend some time just driving around to check out the sights. In the fall you might do a color tour, and during holidays you could check out lighted homes. Or drive through a pretty neighborhood to get landscaping ideas.

15. **Have a spa day**—use the recipes from Day 19 to create a romantic spa date for two. Enjoy a romantic candlelit bath together then take turns giving foot rubs or back massages. Even the most masculine of men would have a hard time saying no to that!

16. **Take a free class**—check out free classes offered by local community colleges, libraries, or retail stores. Shops like Pottery Barn and Williams-Sonoma offer free decorating and cooking classes, while colleges and libraries often have classes available on a variety of topics.

17. **Wash the car together**—nothing says romance like a bucket of soapy water and a nice clean car! Doing chores

together can actually be very meaningful. You get quality time in, plus much-needed tasks get checked off the list—a double bonus!

18. **Explore a nearby tourist town**—is there a popular town nearby that you've never visited, simply because it's "just a tourist trap"? Stop by the visitor's bureau or chamber of commerce for some informational brochures, then spend the day taking a mini vacation in your own backyard.

19. **Attend a local drum circle or jam night**—many parks and beaches host jam nights or drum circles where local musicians, both professional and amateur, get together and just play. It's generally open to anyone and you don't have to play an instrument to simply sit and listen.

20. **Go foraging**—check out a book on foraging for mushrooms, ramps, leeks, fiddleheads, and other edible finds, and go on a hunt! You'll be surprised at what you can discover in parks and woods.

21. **Park**—I'm not talking about that kind of parking (although that could be fun too!); I'm talking about actually going to the park. If you have dog, check out the local dog park. Try Frisbee golf at a local disc golf course, as most are free. Even channel your inner kid by sitting on the swings and talking.

22. **Catch a game**—maybe you can't afford NFL or MLB tickets, but you can check out a local high school basketball or football game. Cheer on your team and relive his glory days under the Friday night lights. It might take you right back to high school.

23. **Race each other**—if you both like to run, head out for a jog together. If walking is more your speed, just stroll around the neighborhood, hold hands, and talk.

24. **Go for a spin**—break out your bicycles and go on a little trip around the neighborhood. You don't have to aim for the Tour de France. Take it slow and enjoy the scenery. Have a destination in mind, or simply go for a random trip through your city.

25. **Take a walk down memory lane**—dig out the scrapbooks and old photos and remember things you've done together. For even more romance, reread cards and love letters. If you're feeling inspired, put away some of those precious memories in a time capsule that you will dig up in ten, fifteen, or twenty years. Talk about romance!

26. **People watch**—remember when you and your spouse were full of inside **jokes?** Sit on a bench in a busy area or mall and people watch. Make up stories and just observe.

> One thing we like to do when my parents have the kids is to go to Barnes and Noble and just explore. We love reading, so it's just so fun to go and get lost in all the books. Then we head to the cookbooks since we both love to cook and get inspired with new recipes. —Claire

27. **Get artistic**—guys can be surprisingly creative. What does your husband enjoy? Model building? Drawing? Painting? Figure out how to scratch that creative itch and try making something together. Not only will you bond, but you'll have something fun to show for it.

28. **Get dirty**—just like washing the car together, doing yard-work can also be pretty fun. Pick a patch of your yard that needs a little weeding or tidying up, and do it together.

29. **Take a nap**—quite honestly, sometimes when you have a babysitter, it's nice to just have a little uninterrupted time together, even if it's just snuggling up on the couch for a nap.

Great ideas! When my husband and I first got married we were pretty broke, and one of our favorite weekend adventures was looking at model homes. It was fun to see how the houses were decorated, and it gave us something to do that was free on an otherwise boring weekend.
—McKenzie

Today's assignment? Plan a fabulous free date night for you and your honey!

Have fun, you crazy kids.

Day 27: Have Fun with Your Family

Believe it or not, we are rapidly approaching the end of our 31 Days. How have you done? Can you believe you've made it for almost four weeks without spending?

To celebrate, I think it is high time we plan a little family fun. Even if your kids are great at entertaining themselves, by Day 27 of the challenge they're probably starting to get just a little antsy for activities and fun! I was surprised at how well my kids adapted to the challenge. They really were on board and helped keep me on track. Still, it's not always easy on the kids, and if your experience has been anything like mine, I'm sure you've had to say no more than a few times.

There are plenty of free activities you can do as a family. In fact, kids have the best imaginations and creativity and can be satisfied with very little. I've seen my girls play dollhouse with homemade furniture and Barbie dresses made out of Kleenex ... for hours. To kick-start your planning, though, check out this list of ideas for free family fun.

25 Ideas for Free Family Fun

1. **Play a "chore cards" game**—okay, so maybe doing chores doesn't scream "family fun," but this is actually a great way to get your kids to enjoy participating in housework. Take a

deck of cards and write one chore task on each one (i.e., unload dishwasher, vacuum living room, dust bookshelves). Gather your family members at the table, shuffle the cards, and deal them to everyone until there are none left. The cards in each person's hands are the chores they must do, but everyone is allowed to trade cards (and tasks). The first person to finish all their chores wins!

2. **Build with Legos**—most kids love Legos, but even more so when their parents join in the fun. Working together to build something big, like a castle or a city, is a lot of fun and helps your kids improve their construction skills by learning from you.

3. **Play hide-and-go-seek**—our family has had some of our best and funniest moments playing this simple game. It works indoors or out with all different ages. Be warned, though—it can go on for hours!

4. **Rake leaves or do other yardwork**—working outside together as a family can be incredibly satisfying. Get your kids to help rake leaves, then have fun jumping in them together. Shovel snow during winter, or plant flowers together in the spring. In the summer, watering the garden can turn into fun running through the sprinklers!

5. **Play board games**—age-appropriate board games are a great way to spend an afternoon. Added bonus? Teaching your kids all sorts of important and essential life skills such as problem solving, sportsmanship, math, reading, and more! Our current favorites include Candyland, Cootie, and Qwirkle. Keep your eyes peeled at garage sales, or ask friends of older children if their kids have outgrown any games.

6. **Do a puzzle**—depending on your kids' ages, break out a "hard" puzzle—100 pieces or more—and spend a few hours working on it together.

7. **Have a movie night**—nothing makes my kids happier than movie night. We get all the sleeping bags, blankets, and pillows in the house and build a comfy nest on the floor. We then pop popcorn and make hot chocolate and settle in to watch our movie of choice. (The local library has a great selection of kids' movies you can check out for free!)

8. **Build a fort**—grab some old blankets and sheets and spend the afternoon creating a super cool hideout with tables, chairs, and other furniture. Or build an outdoor fort with brush, branches, leaves, or rocks. You can even add some Christmas lights for extra ambiance.

9. **Go to the beach**—the beach is a lot of fun whether it's hot and sunny or not. Collect shells, run from waves, build a sand castle, or dip your toes. If you don't live near the ocean, try a river, lake, or pond. Explore the water and see what you can find!

10. **Make homemade Play-Doh**—let the kids help with the process of making Play-Doh (find a recipe here: http://musings-fromasahm.com/2012/02/easy-homemade-playdough-recipe/), and then spend the afternoon making your own dough creations. Use a rolling pin and cookie cutters for even more fun.

11. **Have a cooking decorating contest**—let the kids help with the baking, then gather a variety of icing and other cookie decorating supplies and see who can come up with the most creative design. Award prizes for different

categories—most creative, most beautiful, funniest, sweetest, and so on.

12. **Go for a bike ride**—explore an area of town close by your house, or bring your bikes to a popular bike trail.

13. **Do an upcycling project together**—this is a great way to create something useful and teach your kids about recycling and reusing. For ideas, show your kids the awesome upcycling projects from Day 18, then decide what to make. Let them help gather the supplies or check for free stuff on Craigslist, and then get to work.

14. **Do a family art project**—break out the crayons, markers, and paints and a large canvas or paper and go crazy! You could do something more structured like this handprint family tree (http://www.goodshomedesign.com/diy-family-handprint-tree/) or this fingerprint heart (http://www.busykidshappymom.org/share-love-fingerprint-heart-project/), or simply just let your kids lead.

15. **Visit a free museum**—lots of community museums offer free admission days. Check your local chamber of commerce website for ideas.

16. **Do a free craft project at a local hardware store**—both Home Depot (http://ext.homedepot.com/community/blog/free-home-depot-kids-workshop-first-saturday-month/) and Lowe's (http://www.lowesbuildandgrow.com/pages/default.aspx) offer free kids' workshops. Home Depot holds theirs on the first Saturday of the month while Lowe's offers one every other Saturday. Check with your local store for details.

17. **Make a time capsule**—fill a box with mementos from your life right now—pictures, trinkets, letters to yourself, and so on. Then seal your box and either bury it or put it away some place where you won't open it for ten or twenty years.

18. **Make homemade gifts**—making gifts together is a great way to teach your kids about the joy of giving and the importance of giving from the heart, not just giving "stuff." Brainstorm some ideas for useful or thoughtful gifts you can make together and then get busy! See Day 16 for some crafty ideas.

19. **Do a funny photo shoot**—gather dress-up clothes and any crazy hats, scarves, and other funny accessories you can find and set up a photo booth. Take turns taking pictures of each other looking wacky, or set up the self-timer and get some silly family photographs.

20. **Have a Wii Bowling tournament**—break out the old Wii Sports games you haven't played in years and have an old-school family bowling tournament. Make it an event by serving bowling alley inspired grub!

21. **Visit a free local festival**—check out your local paper or community website to find out what free events are happening in or around your town.

22. **Watch a Dock Dogs competition**—if you've never watched these amazing dogs leap off the dock, competing to see who can jump the farthest, then you're missing out! Competitions are free to watch. Check out the Dock Dogs website (http://dockdogs.com) for an upcoming event in your area.

23. **Have a garage sale**—entice your kids to help by letting them keep the proceeds, or promise to use the money for a fun family outing. See Day 22 for more tips.

24. **Go to the library**—most libraries have great kids' sections with books, games, and free events or story time. Many libraries also often host summer reading contests where your kids can earn prizes for the reading they do every day.

25. **Go fishing**—if you don't have the right equipment or know-how, try asking a friend or family member who does to give your family a fishing lesson. Who knows? You might even come home with dinner!

Depending on the ages and interests of your children, you may need to adapt a little. (Teenagers might need different motivation and activities than an adaptable seven-year-old.) Don't let that keep you from having a great time with the whole family!

Just found out we can go eagle spotting for free!
—Lisa

Your assignment today is to spend time as a family doing something totally new that you've never done before. Get creative and find something free that you can all do together!

$\mathcal{D}ay$ 28: Reflection

Wow! Can you believe you're almost done? You made it four whole weeks! That's pretty amazing. I know it's been tough, but you've soldiered through and now you've got just seventy-two hours to go. Woot!

In this past week, we learned ways you can earn a little extra money, and how to tap into your existing resources to barter, trade, and sell items to get what you need. We also had a little fun with a date night and some family activities! I hope you and your loved ones really explored what it means to have quality time together without spending money. How did your kids feel about the challenge?

One of the things I loved about this week was that I really started to think about the sustainability of spending "zero" as a lifestyle. Granted, very few of us can manage to truly spend zero, but many of us can learn to cut back on excess and separate out the needs from the wants.

So often we get caught up in the mentality that buying something or running to the store will solve our problems. We throw money at things without addressing the real issues. We buy entertainment and turn our imaginations off. Doing this challenge really forces you to open up your mind to alternative answers to life's questions of "what to eat," "what to wear," and "what to do." You can get by spending less. And in some (many) cases, less is actually more.

Going without forces us to appreciate the things we do have. It forces us to turn off the television and focus on our significant other. It helps us to haul out the pillows and build a fort with our kids, play games, and use our imaginations.

Those are the memories that will sustain you through life—not how much you had or bought, but rather, the things you did and the way you spent time and appreciated those around you.

With that, I give you your weekly reflection sheet. Take a moment to explore your feelings and what you learned this week as we approach the end of our challenge. Note your highs and lows, and biggest lessons learned. This week was surely unique for all of us. Documenting your experiences will help you review and reflect later—and learn so much more from your experiences.

Overall, I must say: way to go!

I've been most inspired by blogs like yours that keep me motivated when I want to give up. My biggest struggle has been time management and getting enough sleep through this 31 Days series. —Claire

---

WEEKLY *reflection*

What cleaning & organizing tasks did you accomplish?

_____

_____

_____

goals
FOR NEXT WEEK

What blessings have you expierenced this week?

_____

_____

_____

_____

What has been the BIGGEST struggle this week?

_____

_____

_____

Where were you most tempted (or where did you) CHEAT?

_____

_____

_____

notes:

Copyright · Living Well Spending Less, Inc. www.LivingWellSpendingLess.com

week
FIVE

the FINAL
STRETCH
CREATE LASTING CHANGE

Day 29: **Reassess Your Budget**

You're very nearly done, so it's time to kick your feet up, pat yourself on the back, and ... wait. Not yet. We still have a little bit of work to do. I know you've worked very hard—your house is clean, you've probably eaten your way through most of your pantry, and you likely have more than a few creative recipes under your belt. You've fostered your creativity and maximized your resources.

At this point it would be really easy to say, "Yup, I'm done" and walk away, but that's not how this works.

Part of this project is self-discovery, and we need to think about what you've learned on this journey and how you're going to make it stick.

You probably won't keep "spending zero" all the time, but it's time to assess your budget and see where you are. I'm not going to lie. This isn't going to be easy. It's not something that has a quick fix.

Change is hard. Budgeting is hard.

But you can do this! So let's roll up our sleeves and get it done. As I tell my girls, I never neglect to do something just because it's hard. It's the things you work hardest for that will reward you the most.

Today's assignment is to complete our LWSL Cash Flow Budget Worksheet. (http://www.livingwellspendingless.com/budget-worksheet/). This will give you a good handle on where you are and where you're going. We're going to take a look at your expenses and see what you're doing right and what areas you could improve on. Then we're going to set a few goals!

> I mainly keep track of my cash flow. I have budget categories, but I don't monitor them closely. I should, though. —Michelle

What's that? You already have a budget? Well, even if that's the case, there's still work to be done! You could work on reducing your fixed expenses, such as your mortgage, rent, or insurance rates. (Get more advice on how to do that here: http://www.livingwellspendingless.com/2011/07/27/the-beginners-guide-to-savings-week-3/). Or you could work on cutting down your variable expenses, such as your grocery bill, utility expenses, and even how much you are paying for gas and transportation. (Check out these tips for ideas: http://www.livingwellspending-less.com/2011/08/03/the-beginners-guide-to-savings-week-4/)

After these last four weeks, this won't be nearly as hard as you think!

Let's get down to business!

MONTHLY BUDGET

	TOTAL	BUDGETED	SPENT	NOTES
CHARITY 10-15% TOTAL INCOME				
CHURCH | TITHES:				
OTHER GIVING:				
SAVINGS 10-15% TOTAL INCOME				
EMERGENCY FUND:				
RETIREMENT FUND:				
HOUSING 20-35% TOTAL INCOME				
MORTGAGE | RENT:				
TAXES & ASSOCIATION:				
MAINTENANCE & REPAIR:				
UTILITIES 5-10% OF TOTAL INCOME				
ELECTRICITY:				
WATER | SEWER | GARBAGE:				
CABLE | INTERNET:				
PHONE:				
FOOD 5-12% OF TOTAL INCOME				
GROCERIES:				
DINING OUT:				
CLOTHING 2-7% OF TOTAL INCOME				
ADULT:				
CHILDREN:				
DRY CLEANING | LAUNDRY:				
TRANSPORTATION 2-7% OF TOTAL INCOME				
GAS & OIL:				
REPAIRS & TIRES:				
LICENSE & TAXES:				
OTHER:				

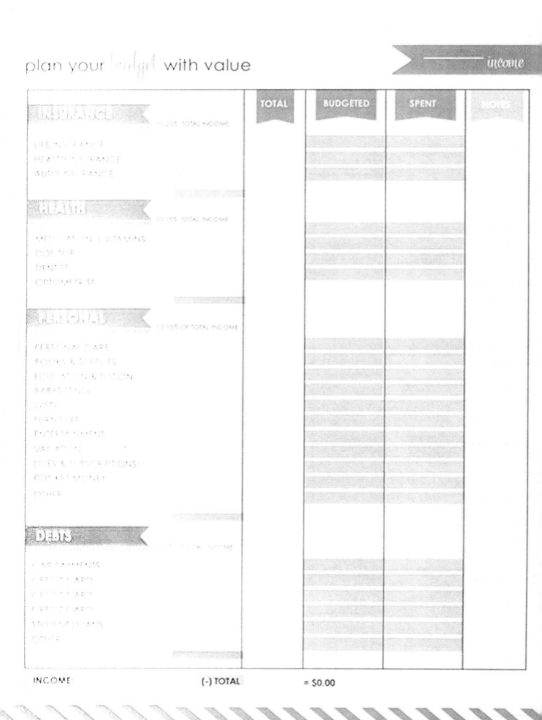

plan your *budget* with value

$Day\ 30:$ Plan for the Future

It's hard to think much about the future when we are busy trying to make it through the day. The future always seems so big, so uncertain—a looming, yet far off, nebulous, sometimes frightening thing. None of us have a crystal ball (at least I don't!), so it's hard to predict what's coming up next.

However, there are always some certainties. You will always have to come up with money for housing, utilities, food, transportation, and the needs of your children. You will probably require healthcare, and you might want to help your kids out with college or wedding expenses. Also, of course, down the road there's retirement.

Even the uncertainties are a certainty—disabilities and accidents can befall anyone at any time, as can sudden unemployment, or even major catastrophes like a fire or flood, or minor ones like a car repair or unforeseen bill. It's not a matter of if, but of when. We need to be prepared.

Assessing your experiences over the past four weeks (all those ups and downs) has helped you reduce your spending short-term. However, the goal of this project is also to start you down the real road to long-term financial peace and safety.

If you haven't already, today's the day to start thinking about how to get yourself out of debt, how to set up an emergency fund, how to start saving, and how to start and contribute to a retirement fund and possibly a college fund.

I know planning for the future can seem like a lot of work, but today I want you to step back and really assess the "why."

Think about why you chose to participate in this journey, and why you should continue. Research ways you can start getting out of debt, and start saving for these big-picture, future investments. Think about how you're going to stick to these spending changes and make them permanent to better set yourself up for a positive future.

Since you already completed your budget assessment and Beginner's Guide to Savings yesterday, you probably have an idea of your monthly expenses. So how can you set up an emergency fund and use any savings and extra income to get out of debt and reach some of your financial goals?
Don't try to tackle it all at once.

As I pointed out yesterday, change is hard. We form attachments to things and habits, but sometimes we have to let go to move forward with positive change. Focus on the true needs of your family and start to make the steps. Assess your debt and find ways to pay down as much as you can. Start saving so that life's little emergencies won't break you or send you further down a debt spiral.

Of course, it's hard to know what the future may hold, but imagine (in an ideal world) how you picture your retirement. How do you imagine your children's education shaping up? Do you have any other expenses coming down the pipeline—braces, care of loved ones (an aging parent, for example), or plans to move, return to school, or change jobs? Once you know what your safety net needs to hold, it's easier to discover ways to build it.

Today's assignment is to gain an understanding of the "why" you are here and to research steps to a positive future. Here are some helpful resources to help you get started.

8 Financial Planning Resources

Get direct links to all 8 resourcers at
www.LivingWellSpendingLess.com/LWSZresources

1. 5 Habits of Successful Debt Slayers (from Living Well Spending Less)
2. How to Not Give Up on Your War on Debt (from Living Well Spending Less)
3. 10 Smart Ways to Build an Emergency Fund (from Living Well Spending Less)
4. Top 10 Ways to Prepare for Retirement (from Dol.gov)
5. How to Save for Retirement on a Low Income (from US News & World Report)
6. How Much Should I Save for Retirement? (from Christian PF)
7. How 401k Plans Work (from How Stuff Works)
8. Guide to College Savings Plans (from CNN Money)

My bank does a rewards program for saving, so every $1,000 you put in your savings per year, you get an extra $50 plus the interest! So I just started a savings account two months ago to pay off student loans. I'm planning to pay off more than the minimum balance at a time so I pay less interest, and by this time next year I'm hoping to have a nice chunk of money to put down on it. —Denise

Familiarize yourself with the terms and ideas surrounding a 401k, retirement savings, college savings plans, and other valuable ways to prepare for the future—even if you aren't sure they are for you, or if they seem unattainable right now. Sketch out an idea of what you want for the financial future of you and your family.

Answer a few questions for yourself, do some research, and start planning for tomorrow—today! Use your newfound zero-spending abilities as a launchpad to reach your ideal financial future.

$\mathcal{D}ay$ 31: What Not to Do Now

Day 31. The end. If you've made it this far, you should feel very proud of yourself. You made it! You survived an entire month of spending zero! In a world where the solution for every problem is to buy something new, you managed to make it an entire month using the things you already had. Way to go!

Tomorrow your zero-spending challenge will be over, and you can go back to spending what you want, when you want. I would like to encourage you to be intentional with how you end this challenge, to put some serious thought into where you want to go from here. To make this your new beginning. You can pretend this challenge never happened, or you can use what you've learned to make some permanent positive changes to your spending habits.

> This month has been so awesome. We have saved so much money and my husband is so happy! I thought it would be hard, and I guess sometimes it was, but mostly it was really motivating! —Denise

After today, you have a choice of two paths: (1) Go straight to the store, credit card in hand, and start swiping, treating yourself to all the things you've said no to all month, or (2) Learn from this past month, apply the principles and ideas you've worked on, and grow toward a place of financial peace.

Option 1 is an immediate "fix." I guarantee you that for a few minutes it will make you feel better. You'll have that high that spending gives you. You'll enjoy your Frappuccino and those new ballet flats and a manicure and lunch at Panera. But then the elation will fade ... and you'll take a look at your bank account and get that sinking feeling of panic that you get when you know you might not make it through the month financially. You'll argue with your spouse and worry about long-term plans for your kids.

Option 2 is the long-term growth plan. No more sick feeling when you look at your bank account! No more fights over money! Commit today to take this momentum that you've built up over the last month and use it to propel you towards a financially stable future. While, yes, you may need to restock your pantry, go to your repertoire of freezer meal recipes and plan out meals for this month, so you can spend much less and eat at home!

> Ruth, I have to admit that I am a little sad that this is the last day of the challenge. I loved all your posts and it's been so motivating and inspiring to read them each day. Although I can't say I followed everything to the letter, it did make me take a closer look at my spending and cut back a lot. —Amanda

Keep speed cleaning your house each day and keep things tidy and in order so you can quickly see what you have on hand. Commit to your closet, and in the future only spend money on items you truly need that are quality made and will last. No more buying simply because it was on sale.

How can you use your newfound abilities to barter and trade for what you need? Think of checking your resources and seeing if you can find an item for free before you run out and buy something. Keep up your meal swaps and trade agreements with friends. Maybe you can trade babysitting, housekeeping, or dog walking. Get creative!

The next time you need a gift, I'll bet you have a few DIY ideas in mind. Think of ways you can give of yourself, rather than resort to another gift card or store-bought item. Learn a new craft and use those skills to create gifts for the next holiday or birthday.

Most importantly, spend quality time with your significant other and your kids. It doesn't mean you need to drop hundreds of dollars on vacations and amusement parks. A simple game day can be just as much fun. Learn to appreciate the little things, nurture yourself so you can nurture others, and understand that giving up on spending doesn't mean giving up on all luxury or happiness.

Post-Challenge Dos & Don'ts

DO review your finances at this point. Compare what you spent this month with previous months. The first time my husband and I did this challenge we were absolutely shocked to discover that we spent less during our challenge month than in any other month in our marriage. Seriously.

DON'T run out and buy everything you wanted during the challenge. Just as I said above: I know you want to, but don't. Give it a day or two before you run to the store. Make a list. Think about the things you really need versus what you want.

DO carry these lessons forward as you plan your budget for the future. Consider upcoming holidays, birthdays, and vacations, and make accommodations, but ask yourself if there are ways you can save—things you can make or trade for, or if there's a service you can give rather than a gift.

DON'T run out and restock your entire pantry if you still have food. It's hard to resist the urge, but sit down and make a deliberate plan for the next month. Check what you have on hand, and consider making freezer meals to save time and money. Rather than running to a restaurant, buy the ingredients to make the dish you're craving. (Go ahead—make those cheddar bay biscuits rather than taking yourself out to Red Lobster.)

DO consider some new ways to save at the grocery store. If you take away anything from this challenge, hopefully it's that you'll eat at home a little more and go out just a little less. That alone will save you a bundle. Planning careful trips to the grocery store and using coupons to save money can really help to stretch your budget.

DON'T forget to get creative and have fun! Refashion your clothing, eat out at home, get fearlessly crafty, and enjoy yourself. Having a good time doesn't need to cost you, and in fact, sometimes it can be more fun to spend less. You'll feel the satisfaction of being resourceful and of creating something you can be proud of!

DO consider revisiting this challenge again. My husband and I regularly practice no-spend months, and doing so has changed our lifestyle and way of thinking. Deliberately not spending actually becomes kind of fun!

> This has been amazing, resourceful, helpful, life-changing, and totally awesome! Thank you for sharing this with us. You have truly changed my mindset and my life view. God bless! —Peggy

Congratulations—you did it!

post-challenge
DOS & DON'TS

DO Review your finances at this point. Compare what you spent this month with previous months.

PREVIOUS *months*:

NO SPENDING *month*:

SAVINGS *difference*:

DO Carry these lessons forward as you plan your budget for the future. Consider upcoming holidays, birthdays, and vacations, make accommodations, but ask yourself are there any ways you can save?

big

FUTURE *expenses*:

WAYS TO *save*:

DO Consider some new ways to save at the store. If you take away anything from this challenge, hopefully it's that you'll eat at home a little more and go out just a little less. That alone will save you a bundle. Planning trips to the store and using coupons to save money can really help to stretch your budget.

SAVINGS *to look for*:

DO Consider revisiting this challenge again. Deliberately not spending actually can become kind of fun!

Copyright © Living Well Spending Less, Inc. www.LivingWellSpendingLess.com

post-challenge
DOS & DON'TS

DON'T Run out and buy everything you wanted during the challenge. Take some time to make a list. Think about the things you really need versus what you want.

NEED *lists*

WANT *lists*

DON'T Run out and restock your entire pantry if you still have food. It's hard to resist the urge, but sit down & make a deliberate plan for the next month.

 MEAL *ideas*

DON'T Forget to get creative and have fun! Refashion your clothing, eat out at home, get fearlessly crafty, and enjoy yourself. Having a good time doesn't need to cost you, and in fact, sometimes it can be more fun to spend less.

CRAFTY *ideas*

DON'T Forget to share your challenge results on Instagram, Twitter, or Facebook using hashtag #31DaysLWSZ so that others can share in your journey.

Online Resources

This book and challenge includes many printable worksheets, as well as many links to additional resources online.

To make access to these resources as easy as possible for you, we have set up a page on LivingWellSpendingLess.com where you can find all the links and download information in one convenient place. To access this page, simply go to the following URL:

www.LivingWellSpendingLess.com/LWSZresources

CPSIA information can be obtained at www.ICGtesting.com
Printed in the USA
BVOW02s0910240116

434042BV00041B/2164/P